Teaching Writing Skills

A global Approach

John Benegar

CENTER FOR TEACHING INTERNATIONAL RELATIONS

Second Edition

Printed in the United States of America
ISBN 0-943804-31-0

For further information about the other CTIR publications and programs, please call 303-871-3106, or visit our web site at **www.du.edu/ctir**.

CTIR Publications

BRINGING THE WORLD TO YOUR CLASSROOM

CENTER FOR TEACHING
INTERNATIONAL
RELATIONS

University of Denver
Graduate School of International Studies

For over 35 years, the Center for Teaching International Relations (CTIR) has published high quality materials on international studies for use in K–12 classrooms. As an integral part of the University of Denver Graduate School of International Studies, CTIR is dedicated to improving public understanding of international affairs.

CTIR materials are designed to provide a balanced presentation of information with the goal of fostering critical thinking about international issues. Our age-appropriate lesson plans are written in conjunction with award-winning classroom teachers and are strategically presented in a modular format from which teachers can choose the most relevant lessons for their specific classrooms. Each lesson is:

- Activity oriented
- Based on national education content standards
- Designed to help students prepare for standardized testing
- Written to incorporate language arts and logical thinking skills

CTIR materials fit easily into a classroom curriculum because they are based on core subject matters such as economics, history, civics, geography, and science. By addressing these subjects in an international context, students gain both an understanding of contemporary international events as well as the foundations upon which they are based. CTIR materials provide students with tools to successfully navigate an increasingly global environment.

Internet Resources

By purchasing this book you now have access to a new service provided by CTIR. The Lesson Hand-Outs and Activities included in this book are now available in an easy to download format on our website. Instead of making copies from the book, we invite you to download all of the handouts at once.

It's quick and easy to do. Just go to **www.du.edu/ctir**, click on Publications, and select Teacher Resources. After filling in your name you will be directed to a list of all CTIR books from which you may choose from any of the titles that you have purchased from us. From here you will need a password to open the file.

The password for *Teaching Writing Skills* is: **Essay**

(Note: Passwords are case sensitive)

TABLE OF CONTENTS

INTRODUCTION

Overview

Of the three "Rs" the least emphasized is the one in the middle--writing. When writing is taught, it usually consists of mechanics such as punctuation, spelling, sentence construction, and grammar. These are important skills, but there is another more important area of writing that is often ignored--the communication of ideas. The more critical thinking skills of comprehension, fluency, and verbal expression--not to mention creativity--often take a back seat to the so-called basics, which are really "prewriting" skills. Writing, unlike reading, is seen as a means to an end (term paper for English class, job application, a letter home), not as an enjoyable end in itself. The teaching of writing in schools suffers from this imbalance. Learning is seen as a passive process where students' abilities to speak and write are subordinate to their abilities to read and listen. It is the goal of this unit to try to redress that imbalance and to improve the skills needed to make students good, thoughtful writers.

Rationale

All evidence points to writing becoming less important, not more. Many people believe that other mediums such as television, telephones, and computers are rapidly taking over much of the function of writing. More significant perhaps, is that many people do not value writing. For this, schools must share the blame. Writing is seldom encouraged for its creative and "fun" potential; it is often still used as a form of punishment: Write "I will not talk in class" 100 times.

While our need to write in order to communicate is perhaps decreasing, writing's place as a valid form of expression is as important as it has ever been. It will always be valuable in helping students to arrive at an understanding of the world. For example, students will continue to use writing to express their ideas, opinions, and feelings, to interpret written messages, and to arrive at critical decisions about the world.

Writing is an active process--one that allows students to participate and become involved; that focuses on students' personal experiences, feelings, and observations. In addition, writing can reinforce other skills, most notably reading. Good writers are almost always good readers. Writing can help students critically read and evaluate the massive amounts of information they receive both in and out of school. If students interpret these data coherently, the likelihood that they will have the necessary skills to cope with the future will increase.

A Global Approach

Change--and in certain cases rapid change--is a part of life in the modern world. Recently, we have seen the world shrink from a vast planet of separate peoples to a spaceship of "global villages." While this transformation is intellectual in nature, it is no less real in its effects on our behavior.

Many people are now questioning whether education is meeting the needs of a planetary culture and keeping pace with technological growth. The so-called basics--of which writing is one--are certainly subject to the reevaluation process.

This unit starts from the premise that there is a need for global education and global understanding, and that the reinforcement of certain skills and concepts can lead students to a more humane and global approach to the rest of the world. These concepts include interdependence, perception, conflict, cultural awareness, language, and human rights. Therefore, in this unit, students use and practice writing skills as part of their development toward attaining a global perspective. They are both important and necessary to the goal of a holistic education.

Writing is a highly complex act which requires analysis and synthesis on many different levels. Thus, it is an aid to intelligence that can lead to self-development.

To be literate in today's world, with the increasing rate of change, we need to develop the ability to critically think, read, and write about our global society and our role in a changing world.

When and Where to Use These Activities

This unit is designed for teachers of all disciplines. Those finding it most useful will probably be teachers of social sciences, language arts, and creative writing. However, it is hoped others will find applications for this guide, too.

Activities have been developed for use in grades 6 through 12. They can be used effectively in areas such as writing skills, concept development, verbal expression, communication, and perception.

While each activity involves writing and the reinforcement of a skill, it should be remembered that the process of writing is what is ultimately strengthened. In the final analysis, writing should be seen not as a skill in isolation, but as an important way of communicating.

Objectives

To provide teachers with teaching activities focusing on writing skills and creativity useful in the development of a global perspective in students.

To provide teachers with tools and activity models that will reinforce writing skills.

To integrate writing and reading skills in the areas of verbal expression, word meaning, comprehension, critical thinking, and evaluation.

To reinforce prewriting skills through the actual process of writing.

To understand and reinforce skills and concepts necessary for students to function effectively in a global society.

WHY WRITE?

Title: WHY WRITE?

Introduction: With the influence of television and other forms of media, some people are questioning the effectiveness of writing or even the need to write any more. The goal of writing as a form of communication appears to have been assumed, in many cases, by other instruments of expression. In this introductory activity, students explore some of the reasons for the use of writing.

Objectives:

To identify reasons for the use of writing
To support these reasons with examples

Grade Level: 6-12

Time: One to two class periods

Materials: None

Procedure:

1. Ask students to list (either individually or in small groups) reasons why they write. If they have a hard time getting started, tell them to think of some examples of writing and the reasons why they may have been written.

2. Put the students' list on the board. Then have them take the items on this list and categorize them into general groups that would apply universally to writing. (The categories of reasons should include communication, expression, entertainment, instruction, information, description, theory of the world, and so forth.)

3. Have students bring in examples of the written word that show these reasons for writing. For example, communication--letter, diary; personal expression--political speech, lyrics; entertainment--novel, comic strip; instruction--textbook; information--newspaper, magazine.

4. Have students compare their examples. Do any of them overlap and have more than one use or function? What role do forms of expression play in writing? How many ways can something be written? Which form might be the most effective?

Follow-up:

1. Have students compare writing from different cultures. Are the forms of expression and the uses of writing similar or different? Have students bring in examples to prove their point.

Title: TEN SUGGESTIONS FOR IMPROVING WRITING IN THE SOCIAL STUDIES

Introduction: In this section are ten ways to help improve the writing skills of social studies students. These suggestions provide students with specific examples of more effective writing.

Objectives:

To suggest guidelines for improving skills
To identify ways to make writing clear and readable

Grade Level: 6-12

Time: One or more class periods

Materials: Handout #1, "Ten Basic Suggestions to Social Studies Students for Improving Your Writing"

Procedure:

1. Distribute Handout #1 and go over examples with students.

2. Use guidelines for reference when students are doing writing assignments, especially those that involve research projects.

Title: TWENTY-FIVE WAYS TO STIMULATE CREATIVE WRITING

Introduction: One of the areas least stressed in schools is that of creative writing. Long considered the domain of elementary classrooms and advanced English classes, creative writing can be an effective skills-builder in all disciplines. Unfortunately, in the rush to deposit information, schools lost sight of students' creative energies. Thus, their most creative experiences take place outside of school. In an effort to redress that imbalance, here are some ways to stimulate students' creativity in the area of writing.

Objectives:

To increase ability to write creatively
To build on writing skills through the use of creative-writing activities

Grade Level: 6-12

Time: Variable

Materials: Handout #2, "Creative Writing"

Procedure:

1. From the list of ideas on the handout, choose one or more you would like your students to try. Or, pass out the list to students and let them select their own.

2. Go over papers with students.

Teacher Considerations:

It will probably work best to make this activity optional or to allow it to be as unstructured as possible. It is important that students have fun writing and are able to write about what they want. This will encourage them to continue writing in the future. You may use these ideas and variations any way you like. The overriding goal is to allow students to express themselves in as many creative ways as possible.

Brainstorming is an excellent method for generating creative ideas. It might be a good idea to arrange students in small groups and have them brainstorm for possible writing topics. The more ideas that are generated the better. And the wilder the ideas, the better. In brainstorming, all ideas are valid and should not be evaluated.

USING PERSONAL EXPERIENCE

Title: THIS IS YOUR LIFE

Introduction: An effective way to get students involved in writing is to have them write about what they know. In this activity, students take turns interviewing one another and then writing personal biographies, which allows them to write about their personal experiences and those of others. The activity is especially useful as an introduction at the start of a school year.

Objectives:

To become familiar with the personal history of another student
To recognize that each person is unique

Grade Level: 6-12

Time: One class period

Materials: None

Procedure:

1. Have students pair off with one another, preferably with someone they do not yet know too well.

2. Explain that each student is to write the story of his/her partner's life up to the present. Tell students that they are to take turns interviewing each other. They may ask any questions they wish in order to find out as much as possible about their partner.

3. After five to ten minutes have the students switch roles, so that each has a chance to ask and answer questions.

4. Once the interviewing process is over, have each student write a biography of his/her partner.

5. Ask for volunteers to read their biographies to the class.

6. Have a class discussion using the following questions:

   What types of questions did students ask of each other during the interviews?

   List the types of questions on the chalkboard (for example, "when" questions, "where" questions, "how long" questions).

   Why are some questions asked more than others?

Follow-up:

1. Have students list other questions that could be used in writing a biography. Encourage them to be imaginative.

2. Have students examine the multicultural, multiethnic nature of the class. What are the cultural or ethnic roots of class members? What part does culture play in determining our perceptions of the world? Have students make a list of cultural factors that influence behavior.

3. Have students make a list of questions they would use to interview someone famous. What would these questions tell us about that person? Have students write a short biography of a famous person (contemporary or from the past).

4. Ask what the students learned about each other from doing this activity and the debriefing.

Title: PERSONAL TIMELINE

Introduction: Having students write about themselves and their experiences can be a great motivator to writing. Often, the more concrete an experience, the easier it is to write about. In this activity the concept of chronology is reinforced through the exercise of writing a timeline.

Objectives:

To analyze important events in a personal timeline
To develop and reinforce the concept of chronological order

Grade Level: 6-12

Time: One class period

Materials: Sheets of newsprint or butcher paper
Crayons, colored pens, or paints

Procedure:

1. Inform students that they are going to draw a timeline of their lives from birth to the present. Tell them that they are free to draw it in any form they wish but that they should be sure to label as much relevant information as possible.

2. Students should label on their timelines all the important events and experiences in their lives in the order in which they occurred. The timelines should be large enough so that several events could be included in one year if needed.

3. When students have finished, ask them to share their timelines with the class.

Teacher Considerations:

It would be a good idea for the teacher to draw a timeline as well, especially if this activity is done at the beginning of the school year. It is a good introduction and lets students know that teachers have histories too.

Follow-up:

1. Compare timelines for similarities and differences. How many were straight lines that stretched from past to present? Were there any circular ones?

2. What kind of information was placed on the timelines? How many included information such as dates, ages, events, family travel, other people, and feelings?

3. Have students project their lives into the future. Have them write stories based on their projections.

4. Have each student draw a historical timeline of important events in the world since his or her birth. Use this information to study history.

5. Have each student develop a timeline of personal changes that have happened during his or her lifetime. These can be external (family, school, friends) or internal (feelings, values, growth).

Title: GUESS WHO´S COMING TO DINNER

Introduction: Young students identify with many different role models as they grow up. These "idols" span many different age groups as well as types of careers. Young people´s heroes can be found throughout such areas as the family, religion, history, music, entertainment, sports, etc. In this exercise, students will write a story incorporating the people they admire most with the qualities those people portray in their lives.

Objectives:

To practice the basic elements of good writing and story compositions
To identify significant people in society and those qualities which make them admirable

Grade Level: 6-12

Time: One to two class periods

Materials: None

Procedure:

1. Have students make a list of the five people in history (past and present) that they would most like to invite to dinner at their home. These should be the five people they admire most. No reasons for their choices are necessary at this point, but encourage them to think beyond those people who may be currently popular. They should think in terms of those men and women who have been influential in their own lives. (Be prepared, however, for the names of people who are popular with the age group of students that you teach.)

2. Ask students to think about those things they would most like to know about these five people. In other words, what is it that attracts them to these particular individuals.

3. Have students write a story describing what might happen when these five people sit down to dinner at their house. Students should be sure to include some biographical information or explanation about the people they have invited as well as what is discussed at the dinner table. Encourage students to be as creative as possible and give some insights as to why they feel the people they chose are important to them.

4. Collect the stories and post them anonymously around the room (or read them out loud to the class) so students can compare each other´s imagined experiences.

5. Discuss with class what kind of qualities they look for in a person they admire.

   Why were some groups of people included in the lists (such as musicians, entertainers, sports figures) and others (like politicians) left out?

   Ask students if their heroes have changed over time?

   Why do they feel this happens as one grows older?

Title: A DAY IN THE LIFE . . .

Introduction: One of the best ways students learn about other cultures and lifestyles is by comparing their own experiences with those of others around the world. Young people especially are curious about those in other countries who are their own age and the way in which they live. This interest in others can be used as a basis for cross-cultural understanding and communication. In this activity, students participate in a short cross-cultural comparison of their daily lifestyles.

Objectives:

To compare and contrast student lifestyles and daily activities in the United States and South Korea
To make inferences about the customs of two different societies
To better understand a culture that is different from their own

Grade Level: 6-12

Time: One class period

Materials: Handout #3, "A Day in The Life . . ."

Procedure:

1. Ask students what kind of information they think they could gather about another culture by looking at a schedule of a typical student's activities for a single day in his/her life. What kind of things could you say about that student's habits and customs relating to work, school, recreation, etc? What might this data tell us about his/her society, family life, education, values, etc?

2. Ask students to pick a typical day in their lives and make a chart of their own daily activities, complete with times, for a weekday and weekend. Have them begin with the time they wake up in the morning to the time they go to bed at night. Describe briefly how they spend each day. Tell them to be as specific and accurate as possible.

3. When they finish, ask students to share some of their daily schedules for weekdays and weekends. Ask them what assumptions they can make about U.S. society from this information. Write these on the board.

4. Next, distribute Handout #3 (or make a transparency). Tell students they are seeing a schedule of activities for a weekday and a weekend of a "typical" 11th grade student in South Korea. Ask: What sort of

assumptions can you make about life in South Korea after viewing this information? List responses on the board.

5. Ask students to compare their own schedules with that of Sungsoo Lee of South Korea. What kinds of similarities or differences exist in the two schedules? What can this information tell us about American and Korean societies as it relates to young people? Who seems to have it easier in terms of time commitments? Recreation? School work?

6. Compare the two lists on the board. Ask students if they wish to change any of their ideas about Korean society? American society? What values seem to be most important in each culture? Revise the lists to more accurately portray each society as they think it really exists.

Follow-up:

1. Invite a guest speaker from another culture (a foreign exchange student) into your class to help students check out their assumptions concerning differences between two cultures. Prepare interview questions in advance to ask the speaker about his or her culture. These should deal not only with the way of life in another culture, but also how that person feels about his or her experience of American culture.

2. Use letters written to foreign pen pals as a basis for explaining the stereotypes we create about other cultures.

3. Using Culturgrams,* find out more about South Korea's customs and cultural patterns. Then make one for the United States that would explain to Koreans something about our culture.

*Culturgrams are four-page briefings covering customs, manners, and lifestyles for 102 different countries. They are revised and updated periodically. They can be purchased from Brigham Young University, Kennedy Center for International Studies, Publication Services, 280 HRCB, Provo, Utah 84602 (801) 378-6528.

USING PERCEPTION

Title: TRUSTING YOUR SENSES

Introduction: One of the school system's greatest weaknesses is its failure to fully develop students' sense experiences. As students grow older, more emphasis is placed on the sense of sight and little or none on the senses of touch, hearing, taste, or smell. Traditionally, writing is approached through sight at the expense of a wealth of sensory data. In this activity, students have the opportunity to explore their other senses and use that experience as material for their writing.

Objective:

To explore sense experiences for students
To utilize specific sense experiences as bases for student writing
To encourage writing using observations based on sensory experiences

Grade Level: 6-9

Time: One class period

Materials: Blindfolds
Something to taste, something to smell

Procedure:

1. Begin activity using a sense students are most familiar and probably most comfortable with--sight. Have the class list all features and qualities of what they see inside the classroom, e.g., desks, people, paint, and clothes. Then have them do the same for things they can see (or remember) outside the building, e.g., buses, clouds, people, and buildings.

2. Have students look around the room and pick a person or an object to describe. Tell them to study their subject carefully and write down what they see. Often they will see things they never noticed before.

3. Have students close their eyes and listen silently and carefully for one minute (no less). Then have them write down all the sounds they heard.

4. Ask for volunteers to come to the front of the room to be blindfolded. (This can also be done with the whole class closing their eyes again.) Pass several strong-smelling objects (soap, spices, perfume, vinegar) under the subject's nose. Ask the student to identify what he or she is smelling.

5. Ask for more volunteers (or the whole class can participate); pass around something to taste (sweet, sour, salty, bitter, smooth) and have them identify what they are tasting.

Follow-up:

1. Students should now be more in touch with their primary senses and better able to use them in writing. Have each student write a short piece that appeals to one or more of the senses specifically and concretely. Give good literary examples if necessary.

2. To show the power of the senses use the following variation of steps 4 and 5. While the subjects are blindfolded, have them taste a food (apple or potato is best) while holding an onion under their noses. Ask them immediately what they are tasting. Then discuss the power one sense has over the other (in this case smell over taste since subjects will think they are tasting onions) and over thought processes. They can then begin to look at how dependent we are on certain senses like sight to the exclusion of others.

Title: EVERY PICTURE TELLS A STORY

Introduction: Visual stimuli can be a strong component of writing. Reporters, poets, and artists are people whose jobs depend on it. Anything in the students' environment can be a subject for writing. In this activity, students first collect pictures (visual stimuli) and then add the written word to describe or tell a story about what they see.

Objectives:

To use visual cues such as pictures to write a story
To write a story using pictures in sequence

Grade Level: 6-12

Time: Two class periods

Materials: Magazines or Polaroid cameras
Colored paper
Markers or crayons

Procedure:

1. Tell students that they are going to be writing stories that they themselves will be illustrating. Since you will have a limited number of Polaroid cameras, students will have to take turns or work in small groups. Have them go out around the school and take a series of pictures. (You can structure this to meet your own objectives.) Have them take pictures at random or in sequence to show cause and effect, past and present, or time lapse.

2. If cameras are not available have students cut pictures from magazines, or use photographs. Or, cut out a series of pictures from magazines and have students write stories based on a single theme or title such as "Day in the life of ______ ______" or "The strangest thing happened on my way to ______."

   Have students outline and write stories to fit their pictures. Encourage them to be creative. (The writing may take two class periods or can be continued at home.) The pictures could also be mounted on posterboard with stories attached.

3. After students have finished their stories they can share them with the class using their pictures as illustrations. If students have written stories showing cause and effect, others can evaluate the stories and pictures together.

Follow-up:

1. Have students write their own captions for pictures in newspapers or textbooks.

2. Have students cut out pictures from current newspapers or magazines and write news reports describing the action. Students could also tell the story from two different or opposing perspectives in order to influence their audience.

Title: A SYMBOL OF THE TIMES

Introduction: Students become aware at a very early age of the importance and necessity of symbols in their lives. From the familiar shape and color of a stop sign to the logo for the latest popular product, symbols appear in all facets of our lives. Students need to know the various uses for symbols as well as the fact that they can change to meet the shifting demands of society. In this activity, students will design new symbols for existing institutions.

Objectives:

To define the meaning of symbols
To assess the different uses and purposes of symbols
To design symbols that will communicate a message to other people

Grade Level: 6-12

Times: One to two class periods

Materials: Butcher paper (optional)
Construction paper
Colored pencils, paints, or crayons
Marking pens
Scissors
Rulers

Procedures:

1. Divide class into small groups (three to four students per group) and ask them to make a list of five different kinds of symbols. Student responses might range through such categories as mathematics, politics, religion, grammar, road signs, brand names, etc.

2. Have students post their group responses on the board. (Or have them make their lists on pieces of butcher paper and tape these up around the room.)

3. Discuss the different categories or types of symbols students have listed. Compare them to find commonalities. Ask students: In what ways are symbols used to communicate a message to people without the use of language?

4. Ask students, in their groups, to develop a working definition for symbols. Again, share their responses with the whole class. (A good reasonable definition might be: Something, such as a printed or written

sign, that stands for or represents something else.) To be effective, symbols should also be easily recognizable.

5. Inform students that they have been selected as designers who have been asked to create a design for a new symbol to be used by certain national and international organizations.

6. Give each student construction paper and markers for the next part of this activity. Tell each student that he/she will be able to create and draw his own design.

7. Write on the chalkboard the following list of topics from which each student should choose the one he or she wants to use as the basis for his/her symbol. (Hint: you can make this a group project where students in each group work together on one symbol if you desire. Enough examples are given for several groups to work independently of each other.)

   1. Political Parties - Democratic
      Republican
      Independent
      Communist
      Socialist
   2. American or State Flags
   3. Democracy
   4. Socialism/Communism
   5. United Nations
   6. Family Coat-of-Arms
   7. Consumer Products
   8. Business/Corporation

Follow-up: Have students collect symbols from home, school, TV, newspapers, business companies, etc. over the next week and bring them in to examine as a class. Have any changed over time? If so, why?

Title: A WORD IS WORTH A THOUSAND PICTURES

Introduction: Almost everyone is familiar with the old cliche about a picture being worth a thousand words. It is also true that a single word can conjure up numerous images all on its own. The same word can mean different things to different people based on several factors the listener brings to that word, such as background, experience, perception, and context. In this exercise, students will illustrate global terms to express their meanings in creative ways.

Objectives:

To express the different meanings that words can have based on the context in which they are used
To visually define several global terms and concepts

Grade Level: 6-12

Time: One to two class periods

Materials: Paper
Colored pencils or crayons
Handout #4, "A Word is Worth A Thousand Pictures"

Procedure:

1. Ask students if they can visualize or imagine what a written word might look like if it was based on its sound, shape, or meaning. Ask them if they can think of any examples that might fit this description.

2. On a blank sheet of paper, have students draw an example of such a word and then share the results with the class. (You might want to have some, or all, of the examples drawn for the benefit of the class on the chalkboard so all can see it better.) If the students are having a hard time getting started, you might give them an example. Words such as squeeze, pull, or knot can be easily drawn to look like or emphasize the action the word represents. A simple example might be the word "telephone" with wires drawn in connecting the "t" and the "h" to visually describe the nature of the word.

3. After students understand how to visually portray the meaning of a word, give them each a copy of Handout #4. Tell them you would now like them to visually demonstrate, through their drawings, the meanings of this list of global terms and concepts. Their examples should look like the meanings of the words as they understand them.

4. Again, share students' responses and ask for volunteers to draw their examples on the chalkboard. See if the other students can guess the meanings of the words by just using the drawings themselves. (Let them use dictionaries if necessary, but encourage them to rely on the drawings themselves.)

5. Have students bring in other examples to class the next day. Structure the assignment to deal with certain categories of words such as people, cultures, global concepts, humor, etc.

THE ROLE OF LANGUAGE IN WRITING

Title: IT GETS CURIOUSER AND CURIOUSER

Introduction: A great obstacle to success in writing can be language and grammar. The many written and unwritten rules in the English language often hinder rather than advance the writing process. Students often complain that teachers are more interested in how a written piece looks than what it says. In this activity, students get the opportunity to play around with curious twists and turns of language and discover the role language plays in writing.

Objectives:

To become more aware of language use in the environment
To become familiar with the role language plays in the writing process

Grade Level: 6-9

Time: One class period or longer

Materials: Handout #5, "It gets Curiouser and Curiouser"

Procedure:

1. Explain to students that there are many peculiarities about language that appear in written messages every day. A simple example is one where the same word has two or more meanings as in "bear to the left," or "bear with me," or "a brown bear."

2. Distribute Handout #5. Go over the examples with the students and discuss their literal and implied meanings. (For example, "Slow, Children Crossing" seems to describe a place where slow-moving children might cross a road. The implied meaning, of course, is quite different, telling motorists to slow down as children may be crossing the road.)

3. Ask students, individually or in small groups, to add examples to the handout.

4. Have students share their examples with the class, examining implied and literal meanings.

Follow-up:

1. Make this a homework assignment; ask students to bring in as many examples as they can to class.

2. Discuss with students where these "language curiosities" might be found (e.g., road and traffic signs, restroom walls, advertisements, local colloquialisms).

3. Have students collect examples of other interesting, odd, or curious uses of language.

4. Have a language journal in the classroom where examples of language curiosities can be recorded.

5. Prepare a dictionary of slang words or neologisms either currently in use or out of date. What are some of the factors that cause language to change?

Title: IT WORKS BOTH WAYS

Introduction: Reading comprehension can benefit from writing. Understanding what one reads can improve with the development of writing skills. Good writers are almost always good and avid readers. This activity helps to reinforce reading and writing skills.

Objectives:

To develop word skills
To improve the skills of writing, spelling, and reading comprehension

Grade Level: 8-12

Time: One class period

Materials: Handout #6, "It Works Both Ways"

Procedure:

1. Distribute copies of Handout #6. Explain directions. Students are to find the correct word for each definition. The answer to the first definition in the pair is the reverse of the answer to the second.

2. Have students complete the handout and go over the answers with them.

3. Have students work in pairs or small groups. Make a list of ten pairs of definitions following this same format. Have them make an answer sheet and try out their list on the rest of the class. Make dictionaries available for those students who have trouble getting started or need to check on spelling.

Answers:

1.	pots	stop	8.	yard	dray
2.	dab	bad	9.	tip	pit
3.	don	nod	10.	spin	nips
4.	pin	nip	11.	mart	tram
5.	sleek	keels	12.	loot	tool
6.	part	trap	13.	loop	pool
7.	mad	dam	14.	revel	lever

Answers:

15.	tide	edit	21.	diva	avid
16.	sleep	peels	22.	live	evil
17.	tar	rat	23.	spot	tops
18.	dog	god	24.	spit	tips
19.	reel	leer	25.	bard	drab
20.	deer	reed			

Title: WORD POWER

Introduction: For centuries, words have been thought to contain power in and of themselves, beyond their meanings. The very sound of words, for example, in a religious ritual, can have an effect on those hearing and making the sound. Words also have the power to evoke emotions and ideas in people just by association. A good example of this is propaganda. In this activity, students use words to create a chain of ideas that can be combined into a written whole.

Objectives:

To compare word associations and meanings
To recognize the relationships and interdependence between different words and concepts

Grade Level: 8-12

Time: One or more class periods

Materials: Handout #7, "Word Power"

Procedure:

1. Distribute copies of Handout #7. Explain that there are words (concepts or ideas) within each circle. Have students write at the end of the arrows words related to or triggered by the central word. Whatever the student associates with the word is valid.

2. After students have completed the circles, have them compare their responses. What words were triggered in their minds and why?

3. Have students write a story about the primary word using all their word associations. Make sure they explain what might appear to be contradictions in their responses. Next, have students write a short story about, or description of, the primary word using all of their new word associations. Make sure students explain what might appear to be contradictions in their responses.

Follow-up:

1. Ask students if they can define their reasons for word associations. Were they emotional responses or purely random choices? Which has more power to make us act, appeals to emotion or appeals to logic?

2. What is the role of perception in the process of word association? How does it influence our behavior? How is this related to the power of propaganda?

3. Are some words more powerful than others? What makes a word "powerful"? Is the meaning of a word always more important than the association it evokes? Think of instances where the emotional appeal of words has overruled their meaning.

4. What is behind the power of an "idea"?

Title: GLOBAL DICTIONARY

Introduction: Children learn at an early age that the same word can have several different meanings or uses. There are many such words and concepts in the English language which depend on context clues for their meanings. In this activity, students are introduced to some global concepts which can have very divergent meanings and applications in everyday life.

Objective:

To recognize context clues in decoding a word or concept
To differentiate different meanings from words and concepts
To become familiar with common global terms and concepts

Grade Level: 6-12

Time: One to two class periods

Materials: Handout #8, "Global Dictionary"
Student dictionaries

Procedure:

1. Begin this activity by asking students if they can think of any common words or terms that might have more than one meaning, based on how it is used in a sentence. (Remind students that many such words change meaning dramatically when used as a noun or a verb.) Examples might be words such as fire, face, bear, chart, grave, match, mind, place, round, etc.

2. Explain the importance of context in deciphering the meaning of a word. Also demonstrate that even though the word in question may be new or unfamiliar, the surrounding clues can be useful in decoding the definition of that word.

3. Give each student a copy of Handout #8. Make student dictionaries available so students can look up the new words in this activity, if necessary. Have them find out at least two different meanings for each word listed on the handout. Then have them use the word in a complete sentence to express each of those different meanings. (This part of the activity might be given as a homework or research assignment in which case parents, teachers, and other students might be used as sources of information.)

Follow-up:

1. Have students research the origins or etymology of these words to see where they came from and what are their literal meanings in another language. This could open up a discussion of how words developed in our own language and how their meanings have changed as society evolves.

2. Have students look for key words and terms in a newspaper or magazine, cut them out, and bring them into class. Post them around the room and analyze how they are used in various contexts. Keep a scrapbook of these terms throughout the year.

3. Have students make a global dictionary of their own, showing all the different meanings their words could have. Have them illustrate the definitions of these words in some way.

Title: THE TERMINOLOGY OF DEVELOPMENT

Introduction: One of the most important skills in the area of concept development is that of definition of terms. Students need to be aware that a concept can have several different definitions or interpretations. Specifically, terms we select to describe other nations or parts of the world often influence our perceptions of those countries and peoples. So it is important to carefully examine the terms that we use to categorize, especially when dealing with the areas of social, economic, and political development. In this activity, students can see that names and labels do influence our perceptions of the world.

Objectives:

To examine terms used to categorize parts of the world
To define the term development as it applies to global society

Grade Level: 9-12

Time: One class period

Materials: Handout #9, "Terminology of Development"
Handout #10, "Map of World"

Procedure:

1. Tell students that they are going to look at some names and labels that have been used to describe and define the world. Discuss with them the importance of perceptions in forming their own view of the world.

2. Distribute Handout #9. Go over the terms with them, explaining that these have been used to describe nations in various stages of comparative social, economic, and political development.

3. Have students add to this list any terms they know of which further delineate the world on the basis of some kind of development pattern.

4. Using Handout #10, have students take one of the pairs of terms from their list (such as developed/undeveloped) and identify those parts of the world that fit that description. This may involve some additional research on the part of students to determine what is meant by each of the terms.

Follow-up:

1. Using a map of the world, have students identify those parts of the world that are defined by the terms on their lists.

2. Begin to define the term development. Students should be allowed to come up with their own conclusions. But they should also be made aware of all the factors which make up such a complex term, such as society, government, economy, culture, etc.

3. Students can critically evaluate the list of terms. They should look at the role that labels, stereotypes, generalizations, and categorization play in determining our perceptions of the world and ourselves.

4. Research the origin of these terms. Are they labels which people in other countries have chosen for themselves? If not, why not? How do people in the Third World see their place in the world?

5. Have students decide which, if any, is the most accurate term to describe the world. What are their reasons for choosing the term they did? What are some of the obstacles in deciding on such a term?

CLARITY IN WRITING

Title: REWRITING HISTORY

Introduction: Among the most well-used documents in social studies are historical documents. Since they are subject to the limitations of time and culture they often reflect a specialized vocabulary. As students are required to become familiar with these primary sources, they need to be able to read and comprehend this language. In this activity, students compare excerpts from American historical documents and rewrite them for their grade level.

Objectives:

To compare and contrast American historical documents related to independence and government

To assess comprehensibility of certain materials

Grade Level: 9-12

Time: One class period

Materials: Handout #11, "Rewriting History"

Procedure:

1. Explain to groups that documents are often written by specialists in certain areas so that they contain a very specialized language. The background of the authors (lawyers, professors, politicians, statesmen) also affects the writing style of the document. Have students briefly list some examples of specialized language.

2. Divide class into four groups. Give each group an excerpt from Handout #11.

3. Tell each group to rewrite their excerpt in a form which they themselves can understand. They may want to change the writing style and vocabulary. This is fine as long as they remember to preserve the meaning of the document. Their task is only to make the passage more comprehensible to themselves.

Follow-up:

1. Have students bring in examples of documents or literature that are written either in a specialized language or for a special interest group (teachers, mechanics, engineers, psychologists, nurses). Rewrite them for a mass audience.

2. Take a textbook on United States history (or any other subject) that is above the students' reading level and have the class rewrite sections of it for their grade level.

Title: SAY AGAIN, PLEASE

Introduction: Language plays a key role in the writing process. If students cannot understand the meaning of what they read they are going to have a difficult time determining how it was written. As this activity illustrates, what students know can become unintelligible when the language is changed and unfamiliar words are used.

Objectives:

To identify how language can be used to change the meaning of the written word

To demonstrate students' ability to change word meanings into comprehensible sentences

Grade Level: 9-12

Time: Two class periods

Materials: Handout #12, "Say Again, Please"

Procedure:

1. Tell students that you would like to demonstrate to the class how language can be used to change something recognizable into something they do not understand. Discuss those factors which make it difficult for students to identify the sayings. (Possible responses: the language was too specialized; words were too hard; never heard it that way before.)

2. Divide class into two groups. To one, give a copy of Handout #12, Form 1. To the other, give both Form 1 and Form 2.

3. Have each group read Form 1. Tell the first group that they are to rewrite the statement so that it is understandable to them. Have the second group read Form 2 and write down their comments about how it has improved or changed the first statement.

4. On the second day, have group 2 read their revised statement, Form 2, to the whole class. Then have group 1 read their second statement to the class. Have the groups compare their revised versions. Which one of the two is the clearest statement and the easiest to understand? Which group better understands the meaning of the statements--the one given the revised version or the one that spent time revising it themselves?

5. Discuss with students those factors that make it difficult to interpret written messages. (Possible response: the language was too specialized; words were too hard; never heard it that way before.) What possible reasons might someone have for using language that is so hard to understand?

Follow-up:

1. Have students bring in examples of writing that is hard to understand because of the reasons listed above. A good example might be a document only a lawyer could understand.

2. Have students take an item written in specialized language or jargon and rewrite it to make it recognizable to others.

3. Have students rewrite a slang expression, a proverb, or a popular saying (as in an advertisement) so that others could understand what is meant.

4. Have students rewrite passages from higher level textbooks, so that they can better understand them.

Title: TRUTH IN ADVERTISING: FACT OR FICTION?

Introduction: Some of the most subtle and powerful techniques of propaganda are no longer the exclusive domain of governments. They now reach us daily through the medium of advertising. By now we are all familiar with the varied, and often conflicting, appeals to buy: be different, be part of the "in" crowd, be a success, more is better. Students can be especially vulnerable to such influences. In order to understand this process, students need to develop the skill of discrimination of fact and opinion to decide if there really is truth in advertising.

Objectives:

To discriminate between facts and opinions and half-truths
To recognize propaganda techniques in advertising
To observe the appeals made by advertisers on the basis of age group, sex, peer pressure, and implied need

Grade Level: 6-12

Time: One class period

Materials: Handout #13, "Truth in Advertising?"

Procedure:

1. Ask students to identify some of the more popular commercials they have seen on television or in magazines. What are the advertisements trying to convince people of? To sell? How do they go about it? Have students list some ways advertisers try to get people to buy their product. (Jeffrey Schrank in his book, DECEPTION DETECTION, lists some of the following ways in which advertisers push their products: unfinished claims, different and unique claims, vogue claims, band-wagon the customer, and rhetorical questions.)

2. Give each student a copy of Handout #13. Ask them to find out what is wrong (if anything) with each advertising claim. What propaganda methods are used to sell the product?

3. Have students rewrite the inaccurate ads to make them more truthful.

4. Have students read their new versions of the ads and compare the changes they have made.

Follow-up:

1. Have students bring to class other examples of propaganda techniques. These could include political campaigns, ideologies, special interest groups (Ku Klux Klan, American Nazi Party, Palestinian Liberation Organization, Jewish Defense League), and others.

2. Have students research the historical origins of propaganda. What are its purposes and uses?

3. Another use of advertising is the reinforcement of existing perceptions and stereotypes of other people. Get students to document the presence of stereotypes and sex roles in advertisements. Have them rewrite the ads to eliminate sex role and cultural stereotyping.

4. Compare identical products and find which ones compete with each other yet are produced by the same company. Compare prices and advertising claims.

5. Jeffrey Schrank lists excellent ways to seek out deception in the market place.

   A. researching honesty-in-labeling in food products--naming foods according to their true ingredients.
   B. listing euphemisms and sound-alike words used by the food industry to deceive customers.
   C. writing a guide for shoppers listing the most often used additives in foods.
   D. study claims made for drugs and medicine sold over the counter.
   E. evaluate the food business and real estate, and travel sections of your local paper on the basis of consumer information and advertising.

PERSPECTIVE AND WRITING

Title: WRITING MAKES A DIFFERENCE

Introduction: The same subject can be treated in different ways, depending on the perspective of the writer. An event such as a car accident or an incident like Watergate can have several different, often conflicting, interpretations. Cultures with dissimilar customs and histories are often subject to misinterpretations and ethnocentrism when they are written about from outside their culture. There is a tendency to impose one's own values and standards on another culture when writing about it. In this activity students compare writings on a unique cultural custom to detect cultural bias and differences.

Objectives:

To recognize cultural bias in writing
To compare writing styles of different authors on a similar subject or theme
To compare writers' treatment of values as they relate to cultural customs

Grade Level: 8-12

Time: One class period

Materials: Handout #14, "Buzkashi"
Handout #15, "Caravans"

Procedure:

1. Pass out copies of the two handouts.

2. Have students read the two excerpts. Handout #14 is an article which appeared in Natural History magazine and Handout #15 is a passage from James Michener's Caravans.

3. Have students compare the two versions they have just read according to the following criteria:

   A. Audience writer is appealing to

   B. Style of writer

   C. Evidence of cultural bias in the writing

   D. Historical background on the subject (origins, rules, etc.)

   E. Discuss which version did the students enjoy more? Why?

4. After students have shared their findings, have them choose a style and write their own stories describing the sport of buzkashi.

Follow-up:

1. Have students edit cultural bias from the excerpts. How does it affect the writing?

2. Have students research the sport of buzkashi and do an in-depth written report on it. Or, get them to investigate another sport while paying attention to cultural and historical origins, social customs, tales, and so on.

3. Show the film "Buzkashi" (available from International Film Foundation, 475 5th Ave., Room 916, New York, NY 10017). This is an excellent film of an actual buzkashi match. Have students compare this media account of the sport with the written version. Which is closer to the truth? Which do they prefer? Why?

Title: PROVERBS

Introduction: People in all cultures have devised oral and written sayings to express their views of the world. When these sayings are passed on over time, they acquire the weight of tradition as well as truth. Such sayings have come to be known as proverbs. Proverbs are usually explicit and concise. But they almost always contain great meaning. In this activity, students will look at proverbs from around the world and compare them with those from the United States.

Objectives:

To compare proverbs of other countries with those of the United States
To recognize similarities and differences between proverbs

Grade Level: 6-12

Time: Two class periods

Materials: Handout #16, "Proverbs"

Procedure:

1. Distribute Handout #16. Have students read the proverbs; then go through them one by one asking students to explain the meaning of each proverb in their own words.

2. Ask students to give reasons for the existence and popularity of proverbs. What is it, exactly, that makes a proverb? Have them begin to define the word. Example: a proverb is a short statement of wisdom or advice that is part of everyday language.

3. Have students list some common U.S. proverbs and read them aloud to the class. How are they similar to or different from those from other parts of the world? What is the subject or theme of each? Get a good discussion going on all the topics proverbs could cover.

4. As a homework assignment, have students collect as many proverbs as they can. Tell them to use other people as resources--parents, neighbors, relatives, friends, teachers. Go over their findings in class and list the proverbs they found on the board. Discuss the meanings of these proverbs.

5. Have students write their own proverbs. Remind them of the universal application of proverbs.

6. Have students share their proverbs with the class. Discuss whether or not they were able to invent their own proverbs. Which ones do they feel were the best?

Follow-up:

1. Have interested students research the history and origins of a proverb and report back to the class. A question they might want to look into is whether there is more than one proverb to express the same idea. Or, are there two proverbs which say exactly the opposite things? For example, "haste makes waste" and "he who hesitates is lost."

2. Have students use their proverbs in public (around the school, with friends, at home) to see if they gain acceptance by other people.

3. Make posters or signs of the new proverbs and place them around the room. This can be an on-going project throughout the school year.

Title: IT MAKES THE WORLD GO ROUND

Introduction: One way to increase students' understanding of the world is by looking at other cultures. By making cultural comparisons in such areas as values, beliefs, lifestyles, customs, religion, and sex roles, we not only learn more about other cultures but also about ourselves. It can provide the opportunity to reexamine our perceptions of the world. In this activity, students make comparisons between marriages in India and the United States.

Objectives:

To compare and contrast marriage customs and sex roles in India and the United States

To compare and contrast social customs and values in India and the United States

Grade Level: 6-12

Time: One class period

Materials: Handout #17, "It Makes The World Go Round"

Procedure:

1. Distribute Handout #17. Have students read it, noting the Indian view of marriage that is presented. Discuss questions at the end of the handout.

2. Have students write a dialogue to present the American point of view concerning marriage. Make sure they write their conversation as if they were explaining marriage in the United States to someone from another country.

3. Ask for volunteers to read their conversations to the class. Have students compare their versions and list their similarities and differences.

Follow-up:

1. Ask students to list possible reasons for the differences in social customs between two cultures.

2. Have students compare the sex roles between women in India and women in the United States.

3. Compare the values Radhika applies in choosing a husband with those important to Heather.

PERSPECTIVE IN THE NEWS

Title: USING THE NEWSPAPER

Introduction: Many resources can be used in conjunction with writing activities. One of the most readily available, as well as least expensive, is the newspaper. Whether a local daily or a newspaper from another city or country, it can be used in numerous ways to stimulate students' writing abilities.

Objectives:

To recognize a newspaper as a creative writing resource
To stimulate creative writing through current events

Grade Level: 6-12

Time: One or more class periods

Materials: Handout #18, "Uses for the Newspaper"

Procedure:

1. Distribute Handout #18 and review it as a class.

2. Have students select ideas from the handout to use with the class. List these suggestions on the board, giving students a choice of examples on which to write.

3. Pass out an assortment of newspapers or sections of a newspaper. Have students complete the writing assignment using the newspaper as their resource.

4. Ask for volunteers to read their assignments to the class.

Title: WRITING AND THE NEWS MEDIA

Introduction: News about the world takes many forms. It is broadcast over radio and television, written about in newspapers, magazines, and books, and is passed on by word of mouth. News, however, is not always an objective matter. It is often distorted or biased or slanted. This can be done unconsciously or knowingly to influence people. Whatever form it takes, news and the media that publicizes it have a profound affect on the world. In this activity, students experiment with writing news from a number of different viewpoints.

Objective:

To recognize that the news can be biased

Grade Level: 6-12

Time: One or two class periods

Materials: Handout #19, "News Items"
Handout #20, "Editorial"
Handout #21, "TV Stations"

Procedure:

1. Explain to students that they are going to write news stories and present them to the class as a news program. Have them break into groups of three or four students each.

2. Give each group a copy of Handout #19 and explain that these are topics for news stories. Also distribute Handout #20 and explain that it is a news item for an editorial.

3. Tell students that each group represents a TV station news team and they will be writing the news from a different perspective. Assign each group a different perspective from Handout #21. Do not let the groups know which perspective each is taking.

4. Have each group choose any three news items to write about from their perspective. They can choose any three they wish, but they should be items that easily fit their slant on the news. The reports should be about one minute in length when they are read aloud. Also have each group write a one-minute editorial.

5. Have each group present their version of the news to the class. They may organize themselves any way they wish. Have other groups guess the perspective from which each was writing.

Follow-up:

1. Discuss with students how easy or difficult it was to slant the news to a particular point of view. How do these perspectives compare with the news they see on TV? Read in newspapers? How objective is television news reporting? Are there other perspectives that could be added to this list?

2. Have students watch a television news program and document the news reporting. Is it objective? Were there news stories that they thought were biased or slanted in some way? Bring results to class.

3. Have students try to write an unbiased, objective news story. Use one of the news items if you wish. What are its advantages and disadvantages? Was it easier or harder to write?

4. Have students follow the same format but this time write a one-minute commercial for a fictitious product (like Crispy Crunchy Cereal). They can use the same perspectives or make up their own. Then have groups make their pitch and have the rest of the class guess what audience that group was appealing to. Have students document the perspectives of ads they see on TV or in magazines. Bring the results to class and discuss them.

5. If your school facilities allow it, try to videotape the students' presentations as if they are actual newscasts. Play back the tape and have students critique the news stories form each perspective.

Title: ON YOUR OWN

Introduction: Perceptions, of course, affect behavior. They also affect the way we see the world and what we write. Even the way we write is influenced by our perceptions. Students bring a myriad of experiences, conceptions, and feelings to their writing. In this activity, students are truly on their own to investigate their own and other people's perceptions and writing styles.

Objectives:

To compare the styles of various writers
To recognize different viewpoints
To become aware of the influence of perception in what is written

Grade Level: 8-12

Time: One to two class periods

Materials: Handout #22, "On Your Own"

Procedure:

1. Inform students that they are going to look at a global issue from a number of different perspectives. (In this case, the example used is the Arab-Israeli conflict in the Middle East.) Explain to them the role that perception plays in determining how we see and relate to the world.

2. Give each student a copy of Handout #22. This is a list of suggestions for writing topics dealing with this global issue. (Depending on the teacher's subject matter, the content may be different but the format can still be followed.) Students are to choose (or are assigned) one of these writing exercises. The purpose is to get students to experiment with different writing styles as well as to examine a controversial subject from several perspectives.

3. Have students share their written work and explain their reasons for their approaches to writing. Brainstorm for more writing ideas.

Title: GLOBAL HEADLINES

Introduction: A prime source of information about the world is still the daily newspaper. Access to newspapers is almost universal now and most events of a global nature are reported in more detail than can be seen on television. As with all good stories, the titles and opening lines should grab our attention and make us want to continue reading. In this activity, students are to read a description of a global issue and formulate a title or headline for each article.

Objectives:

To recognize the value of catching and holding a reader's attention
To participate in creative writing efforts

Grade Level: 6-12

Time: One to two class periods

Materials: Handout #23, "Global Headlines"

Procedure:

1. Ask students how often they look at or read a newspaper--daily, once a week, only on Sunday, rarely, never, etc. Ask them which section or sections of the newspaper they usually read such as sports, comics, world affairs, front page, local and regional news, classifieds, society page, and so forth.

2. Ask students: What is a "headline?" What purpose does it serve? What can it tell us about a particular event or issue?

3. Tell students they are going to be playing the role of a "headline cutter"--a person on the staff of many large newspapers whose job it is to read articles and stories submitted to the newspaper. This person then thinks up headlines that will attract the reader's attention and make him want to read more about it. Each of the short articles the students will be reading concerns a real event or issue of some global or international significance.

4. Distribute Handout #23 to students and have them read each article and write two short, interesting headlines for each one that they hope will grab the reader's attention.

5. When students finish, have them share their headlines with the rest of the class. Discuss their responses. How different or similar were they?

Which ones were the most effective and descriptive headlines? Why? Most original? Most creative? What information did they try to show in their headlines? What point of view, if any, did they establish through the use of headlines?

6. Have each student bring in an article from that day's newspaper (or a current magazine), write a new headline, and then analyze the headline. Were the headlines effective? Accurate? Did they get the reader's attention or not? Did they elicit any specific responses or emotions? Have students use these articles to create new headlines for them that they feel will be more effective.

THE LANGUAGE OF PROTEST

Title: HUMAN RIGHTS POSTERS

Introduction: People use many forms of expression to make their views known. Writing letters, running for political office, starting educational programs, going on strike, or joining protest demonstrations are just some of the ways people express their commitments. Protest posters are a part of most demonstrations. People usually demonstrate because they want others to know their position on an important issue. Posters allow the demonstrators to quickly and succinctly express their point of view. In this activity, students will make posters expressing their views on the issue of human rights.

Objectives:

To stimulate creative efforts that demonstrate an understanding of a particular issue
To become familiar with the function of protest posters
To recognize key aspects of protests
To analyze a poster to determine the perspective of the group using it

Grade Level: 6-12

Time: Two class periods

Materials: Handout #24, "Human Rights Posters"
Newsprint or poster boards
Magic Markers

Procedure:

1. Ask students if they have ever seen or been to a demonstration. Have them explain what it is and why people carry posters or signs. Ask them what can be learned about the people and the cause from reading the posters.

2. Divide class into four groups. Distribute different scenarios from Handout #24. Have each group make appropriate posters. Bring examples from newspapers or magazines. Give students a day or two to think of and look for good poster ideas. It may also be necessary to provide background information about the issues, in this case human rights. The purpose of the activity is to have students identify the key aspects of the problem through making posters.

3. Display completed posters and have each group explain their particular effort.

Follow-up:

1. Have students explore further the issue of human rights. Have them look at related topics such as political prisoners, genocide, freedom of expression, and cultural rights. Have them read "The United Nations Declaration of Human Rights."

2. Change the scenarios to deal with human rights issues in the United States. Are students' posters different or similar when dealing with cases that occur within the United States?

3. Have students meet with others and represent their positions in a discussion much like a Senate committee hearing. The success of such a presentation will depend on the students' background and familiarity with the issue.

4. Change the context and have students make posters dealing with other issues such as the different sentiments between factions during the American Revolution or during the Vietnam War. Posters could depict people's feelings about controversial issues such as taxes, energy, or pollution. The possibilities are endless.

5. Have students write poems protesting or showing their concern for some social condition that they consider unjust.

Title: THE POETRY OF PROTEST

Introduction: When students write, they should experiment. World literature is full of examples of different writing styles and modes of expression. One very expressive but simple technique is poetry. In this activity, students compare the literature of social consciousness movements as reflected in antiwar poetry and poetry about political dissent and human rights.

Objectives:

To recognize poetry as a method of self-expression
To compare and contrast writing styles, forms, and modes of expression
To explore the writing of contemporary political protest

Grade Level: 6-12

Time: One or more class periods.

Materials: Handout #25, "Protest Poetry"

Procedure:

1. Ask students to think of examples of ways in which people express themselves in writing, such as letters, poetry, newspaper stories, posters, graffiti, novels, memos.

2. Explain to students that some forms of expression are more effective than others in conveying a message. There may be several ways of writing about a concept or idea depending on the audience. Ask students if they can think of any examples of writing that appeal to one group over another.

3. Distribute Handout #25. Explain that these poems all deal with political protest or dissent in some way.

4. Have students, either as a class or in small groups, read the poems and compare them based on the following criteria:

   A. What event or situation does the poem describe or allude to?

   B. What is the theme or point of view of the poem?

   C. What is the author protesting in the poem? Supporting?

   D. What is the worldview of the author?

   E. Which poem makes the strongest statement in favor of human rights and why?

5. Have students write poems protesting or showing their concern for some social condition that they consider unjust.

Follow-up:

1. Have students bring into class other examples of writing that deal with political protest and human rights. Get them to bring in as many modes of expression as they can find--narrative, polemic, propaganda, poetry, prose, short stories, biography, historical document.

2. Have students compare the writing of protest over time and cross-culturally to make comparisons from a historical and cultural perspective.

   Some excellent source materials are: Poems of War Resistance, edited by Scott Bates; Poems of Protest edited by Arnold Kenseth; NY: Macmillan, 1968; On Freedom's Side: An Anthology of American Poems of Protest, edited by Aaron Kramer; and In the Time of Revolution: Poems from Our Third World, edited by Walter Lowenfels, NY: Random House, 1969.

3. Collect (or have students collect) record albums containing songs and music from protest movements. These could include antiwar songs, labor movement and unionizing songs, and civil rights marches. Have students compare the theme in the music as well as the language used and historical events mentioned.

STUDENT HANDOUTS

Ten Basic Suggestions to Social Studies Students for Improving Your Writing

Here—briefly stated and with examples—are ten suggestions to improve your writing. You may not be able to use all of them at the same time, for writing assignments vary in purpose. However, these ten guidelines, which are divided into three areas, can assist you to write papers that are stimulating and readable. *Here's to your good writing!*

by Daniel Roselle

Sketches by Robert Diamond

A NOTE TO TEACHERS: This material has been prepared in response to the request of many teachers for assistance in developing the writing skills of their students. It is designed to provide students with specific guidelines for writing effectively. Reprints may be purchased from the National Council for the Social Studies,
Price: Classroom Packet of 15 copies, $3.00 per packet. Please send payment with order, except those on official school purchase order form.

Daniel Roselle, Social Education, Feb. 1977. Used with permission.

AREA I: GOOD WRITING IS CLEAR

1. DO NOT BE PRETENTIOUS. *Express yourself clearly.*

Pretentious

Mary J. Youngquist illustrates pretentious writing carried to an extreme:

"A triumvirate of murine rodents totally devoid of ophthalmic acuity was observed in a state of rapid locomotion in pursuit of an agriculturalist's uxorial adjunct."

Better

Three blind mice ran after the farmer's wife.

••• ••• •••

Pretentious

As Edith Hamilton, distinguished scholar of Greek culture, once pointed out, Abraham Lincoln at Gettysburg did not say:

"That political supervision of the integrated units, for the integrated units, by the integrated units, shall not become null and void on the superficial area of this planet."

Better

Abraham Lincoln did say:

"That government of the people, by the people, for the people, shall not perish from the earth."

••• ••• •••

Do Not Be Pretentious

Pretentious

Many American women accept monogamous connubial relationships

Better

Many American women marry.

2. BE SPECIFIC. *Use concrete words, rather than general terms*

Too General

There are thousands of interesting and unusual organizations in this country. Their names demonstrate that they represent a variety of occupations and professions.

Better

There are over 14,500 national organizations in the United States that represent a variety of occupations and professions. These include: the National Council for the Social Studies, American Cricket Growers Association, Popcorn Institute, Red Suspender League, Dracula Society, National Potato Promotion Board, and Flying Dentists Association.

••• ••• •••

Too General

In the eighteenth century, a symbolic ceremony celebrated the transfer of authority of government from one autocratic ruler to the next. It showed that there was no democracy in the nation, only tyranny.

Better

In 1715 the Duke of Bouillon placed a black feather on his cap and walked out to the balcony of the great palace at Versailles He looked for a moment at the crowd below, which, according to biographer Nancy Mitford, was "curious but not sad." Then he solemnly announced: "The King is dead!" The Duke then returned to the palace, put on a white feather, and went out to the balcony again. This time he proclaimed "Long live the King!" With this symbolic switching of a black feather for a white, the long reign of Louis XIV had ended, and the rule of Louis XV, his great-grandson, had begun. The French people had nothing to say about this transfer of power.

3. AVOID OVERWORKED STATEMENTS. *Express your ideas in fresh and original ways.*

Overworked Statements

- We live in critical times.
- The future is up to us.
- No one can foresee what the future will bring.
- It is time for someone to speak out.
- Science can be used for both good and evil.
- Never in the history of the world has there been such a situation.
- Mankind is at the crossroads.
- The news came like a bolt from the blue.
- There are many burning issues.
- It goes without saying that the nation is in peril.
- The fate of the world is in our hands.

4. DO NOT STEREOTYPE INDIVIDUALS

Stereotyping

The trial jury, which deliberated a third day without reaching a verdict, is a conventional slice of Middle America.

Better

The trial jury, which deliberated a third day without reaching a verdict, includes five housewives, a nurse's aid, a steel worker, a banker, an unemployed painter, a college professor, an engineer, and a chemist.

••• ••• •••

Stereotyping

Men living in the suburbs like to join country clubs, to play golf on Sunday, and to drive sports cars.

Better

George Thompson, who lives in a suburb of New York City, likes to join country clubs, to play golf on Sunday, and to drive sports cars. His next-door neighbor, Robert Shore, shuns country clubs, dislikes golf, and rides the train to work.

AREA II: GOOD WRITING SHOWS RELATIONSHIPS

5. LINK PARAGRAPHS. *Wherever possible (but not always), connect the end of one paragraph with the beginning of the next.*

Example 1

The names of individuals are not always what they seem. Thus, Mother Goose was really a sophisticated Frenchman named Charles Perrault, and not a sweet, silver-haired grandmother who lived in a thatched cottage and wrote her stories by candlelight. Similarly, Joseph Stalin's real name was Iosif Vissarionovich Dzhugashvili.

Link →

This change in Stalin's name is particularly important, for "Stalin" means "Man of Steel." The significance of this fact for the etc.

••• ••• •••

Example 2

A few days after the bomb was dropped on Hiroshima, Russia entered the war against Japan and invaded Manchuria. President Truman again demanded that Japan surrender. When the Japanese did not, a second atomic bomb was dropped, this time on the city of Nagasaki.

Link →

This second bomb struck Nagasaki on August 9, 1945. Five days later, Japan surrendered. In September, the Japanese representative, Mamoru Shigemitsu, signed etc.

6. SET TIME BY PARALLEL EVENTS. *However, remember that this is just one of several ways of setting the time of an event.*

Parallel Timing

Starting about 2,000 B.C.—when the Egyptian civilization was already established, and the earliest Greeks were migrating into the Aegean area—the so-called "Latins" began to move into the Italian peninsula.

••• ••• •••

Parallel Timing

In 202 B.C.—about the time that Asoka's Indian empire was crumbling, and Hannibal's Carthaginians were facing defeat by the Romans—a great new dynasty arose in China. This was the Han Dynasty

Link Past and Present

7. **LINK PAST AND PRESENT.** *However, do not strain to find links that are not really there.*

Linking Past and Present

Why should we study about the ancient Greeks? Are we influenced by them?

We are—if our names are George, Anthony, Dennis, Eugene, Gregory, Homer, Myron, Nicholas, Philip, or Theodore Or if our names are Agatha, Agnes, Catherine, Corinne, Cynthia, Doris, Rhoda, or Thelma. These names are probably derived from the Greek language.

••• ••• •••

Linking Past and Present

Many of our twentieth-century ideas of decimals, minus signs, and numerals may be traced back to India. So can our place-value system of numbers, in which we say 1977 is one thousand, nine hundred, seventy-seven because of each number's place in the figure.

AREA III: GOOD WRITING IS WELL RESEARCHED

8. **USE PRIMARY SOURCE MATERIAL.** *Primary source materials include the direct impression and expression of people living at the time of an event.*

No Primary Source Material

Dr. Martin Luther King was a stimulating speaker. He delivered a speech at the Lincoln Memorial during the Civil Rights March on Washington, D.C., and it moved people greatly.

Primary Source Material

Dr. Martin Luther King was a stimulating speaker. In his speech at the Lincoln Memorial during the Civil Rights March on Washington, D.C., he moved people deeply when he said.

Primary Source Material → "I have a dream that one day this nation will rise up, live out the true meaning of its creed: 'We hold these truths to be self-evident, that all men are created equal'."

••• ••• •••

No Primary Source Material

In 1775 the Foundling Home had the responsibility of caring for thousands of homeless babies. Anyone who visited it said that conditions there were very bad.

Primary Source Material

In 1775 the Foundling Home had the responsibility of caring for thousands of homeless babies. Conditions there were shocking; and Hester Lynch Thrale, an Englishwoman who visited the Foundling Home, wrote:

Primary Source Material → "I saw whole Rows of swathed Babies pining [away] to perfect Skeletons & expiring in very neat Cribs with each a Bottle hung to its Neck filled with some Milk Mess, which if they can suck they may live, & if they cannot they must die."

Use Primary Sources

9. SUPPORT YOUR GENERALIZATIONS WITH EVIDENCE

Unsupported Generalization

Of course, we all know that computers affect everything that we do. No one can argue with this obvious fact.

Supported Generalization

Computers affect our lives in many ways. For example, according to Samuel Zagoria, a member of the National Labor Relations Board:

- A computer in Washington, D.C. is analyzing heart conditions of New England patients via long-distance transmissions of cardiograms.
- At Grand Coulee, computers monitor 420 relay and circuit breaker contacts one thousand times every second.
- Travel at sea is safeguarded by a string of computer-operated Coast Guard lighthouses that detect fog . . . and can even change burned-out lamps if necessary.

Reports from Massachusetts Institute of Technology also make clear the importance of computers.

10. READ

Read as much as you have time for, and then make time to read more! Read—not in order to imitate the styles of others, but to increase your sensitivity to words, to ideas, and to the unlimited possibilities of human expression. Above all, read for enjoyment; and, in time, you may find that your own writing is a source of enjoyment for others.

CREATIVE WRITING

1. Write a biography of the person sitting next to you.

2. Personify some abstract idea or quality (love, democracy, God, beauty) and write about it as if it were a person you knew well.

3. Write down your dreams or fantasies. Pick an object and write down what its dreams might be (an egg, a bottle, an ear).

4. Write the words to a piece of instrumental music.

5. Collect pictures from magazines such as Time, or National Geographic, or a newspaper and write stories to accompany the pictures. Try it with art reproductions and personal photographs.

6. Write captions for pictures.

7. Make a comic book or comic strip.

8. Record all the superstitions they can find.

9. Select a controversial topic such as prejudice, apartheid, war, or abortion and write two essays--one attacking the position, the other defending it.

10. Anti-ads. Write advertisements to get people to stop using a product. Example: "It´s springtime, why spoil it with a cigarette?"

11. Describe a new invention--what does it look like, what is its function (e.g., design a new eating implement)?

12. List or describe the uses for an ordinary object such as an old razor blade, a safety pin, a button, or a newspaper.

13. Develop a word picture describing an abstract quality (brotherhood, peace, poverty, interdependence).

14. Keep a log for a spaceship traveling in the 21st century.

15. Have the teacher give a "sentence starter" and then write a story using it as the first sentence of the story. Or reverse the process and use an ending sentence.

16. Write the history of an event or occurrence that could appear in your autobiography.

17. Choose a famous historical event. Write about what happened in other places either because of or in spite of that event. What was going on beyond the frame of that picture?

18. Keep a journal of your dreams.

19. Find examples of similes and metaphors in poetry. Then write similies.

20. See a movie (without narration or without sound). Summarize what you have just seen or create a narration or dialogue for the film.

21. Write a modern American folk tale; add a moral for good measure.

22. Practice sentence expansion to eliminate ambiguity. Use newspaper headlines as examples. Followup with a story to clarify title.

23. Practice writing different poetic forms such as haiku (three line poem, nonrhyming, usually about nature, 5-7-5 syllable count) or cinquain five line poem, one form following 2-3-4-5-2 syllable count) relating to global issues such as pollution or hunger.

24. Write a description or definition of some common object or idea, then look at what your classmates have written. Put them together to form a class composition.

25. Describe your ideals in terms such as an ideal government, an ideal world, or an ideal friend.

A DAY IN THE LIFE . . .

WEEKDAY AND WEEKEND SCHEDULE OF ACTIVITIES FOR SUNGSOO LEE, AN ELEVENTH GRADE STUDENT IN SOUTH KOREA

WEEKDAY

6:00 - 6:10	GETTING UP
6:10 - 6:20	WASHING & BRUSHING
6:20 - 6:30	CHECKING THE SCHEDULE
6:30 - 6:50	BREAKFAST
6:50 - 7:20	GOING TO SCHOOL
7:20 - 4:55	CLASSES AT SCHOOL
4:55 - 5:25	COMING HOME
5:30 - 7:00	REVIEW
7:00 - 7:30	DINNER
7:30 - 8:30	TAKING A REST
8:30 - 10:30	HOMEWORK & PREVIEW
10:40 - 11:50	READING
11:50 -	WASHING & GOING TO BED

WEEKEND

7:00 - 7:10	GETTING UP
7:10 - 7:20	WASHING & BRUSHING
7:20 - 8:00	JOGGING
8:00 - 8:30	BREAKFAST
8:30 - 9:00	TAKING A REST
9:00 - 12:30	DOING SOMETHING I´D LIKE TO DO; (READING, LISTENING TO MUSIC, WATCHING TV, MEETING FRIENDS, WRITING LETTERS, etc.)
12:30 - 1:00	LUNCH
1:00 - 2:30	SPORTS
2:30 - 3:00	TAKING A REST
3:00 - 7:00	STUDYING
7:00 - 7:30	DINNER
7:30 - 11:40	HOMEWORK & REVIEW

A WORD IS WORTH A THOUSAND PICTURES

Words can sometimes be written in ways that make them look very much like their meanings. Rewrite or draw each of the following words so that it will look like its meaning.

COMMUNICATION

AMERICAN

WAR

PEACE

ENERGY

INTERDEPENDENCE

STEREOTYPE

CHINESE

CONFLICT

OIL

SOLDIER

ENVIRONMENT

HUMAN RIGHTS

COOPERATION

IT GETS CURIOUSER AND CURIOUSER

The following are all examples of "language curiosities." Try and add as many of you own examples as you can.

1. Slow Children Crossing
2. Watch for Falling Rocks
3. No Parking Beyond This Point Enforced
4. Deer Crossing
5. Right Lane Must Turn Right
6. Stop School Bus Loading
7. ______________________________
8. ______________________________
9. ______________________________
10. ______________________________
11. ______________________________
12. ______________________________
13. ______________________________
14. ______________________________
15. ______________________________
16. ______________________________
17. ______________________________
18. ______________________________
19. ______________________________
20. ______________________________

IT WORKS BOTH WAYS

Here are twenty-five sets of definitions. If you get the correct answer for the first definition, simply reverse its spelling and you have the correct answer for the second definition. For example, suppose your definitions were "To spoil" and "A male sheep." The first answer would be MAR. Reverse the spelling and you have the second answer, which is RAM.

A score of twelve pairs is good; fifteen is excellent; twenty is superb; and twenty-three to twenty-five is extraordinary.

1.	Cooking tools	________	________	Cease
2.	Apply gently	________	________	Not good
3.	Put on	________	________	Affirmative head motion
4.	Straight metal fastener	________	________	Catch, pinch
5.	Smooth; stream-lined	________	________	Steel pieces on ships
6.	Portion; separate	________	________	Snare; catch
7.	Angry	________	________	Structure confining water
8.	Play area	________	________	Cart for heavy loads
9.	Gratuity	________	________	Deep hole
10.	Revolve quickly	________	________	Sips of liquor
11.	Shopping area	________	________	Streetcar
12.	Stolen goods	________	________	Implement
13.	Circular structure or line	________	________	Cement enclosure for water
14.	Make merry; delight in	________	________	Bar used as a pry
15.	Rise and fall of water surface	________	________	Proofread
16.	Slumber	________	________	Removes the skin
17.	Road surface protection	________	________	Rodent
18.	A canine	________	________	Deity
19.	Stagger	________	________	Sly look of ill will

20.	Forest animal	__________	__________	Jointed, hollow stalk
21.	Prima donna	__________	__________	Enthusiastic
22.	Dwell; reside	__________	__________	Wicked, depraved
23.	Small mark; specific site	__________	__________	Used with bottoms
24.	Saliva	__________	__________	Extremities
25.	A poet	__________	__________	Dull; lacking brightness

WORD POWER

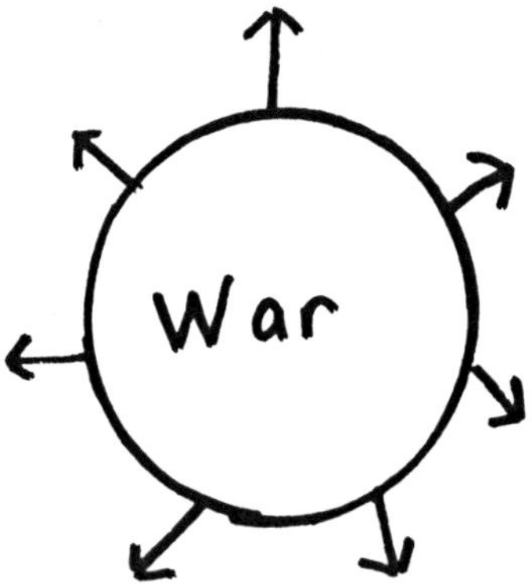

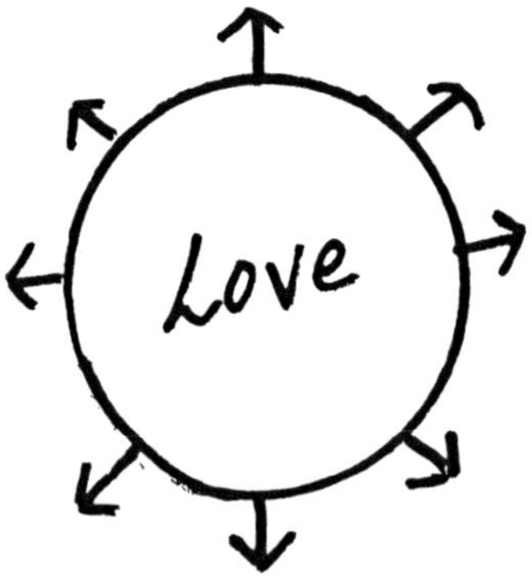

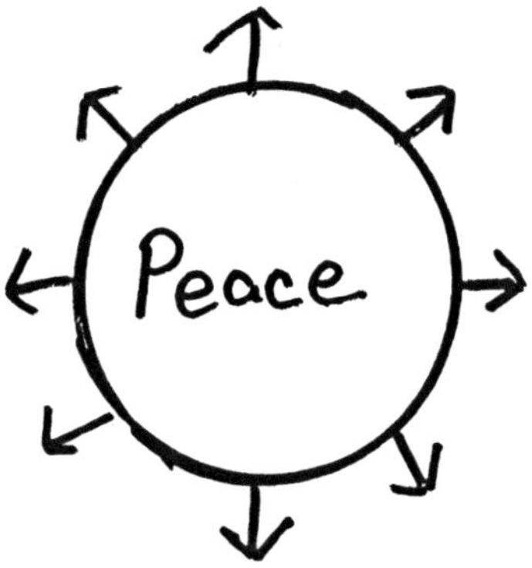

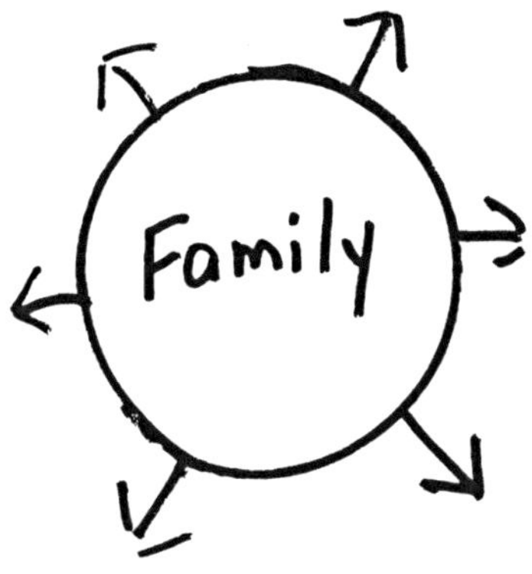
Family

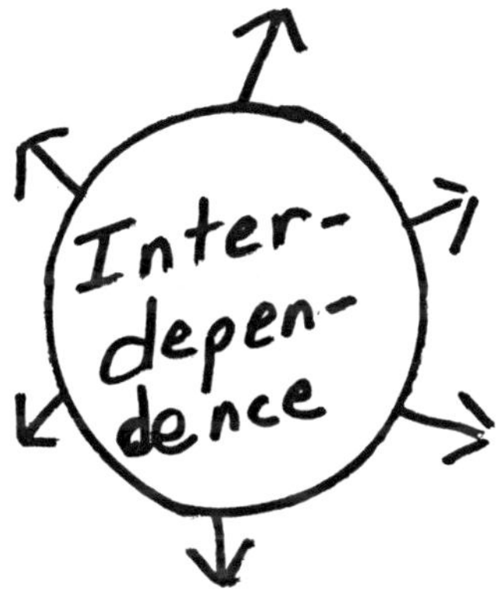
Inter-
depen-
dence

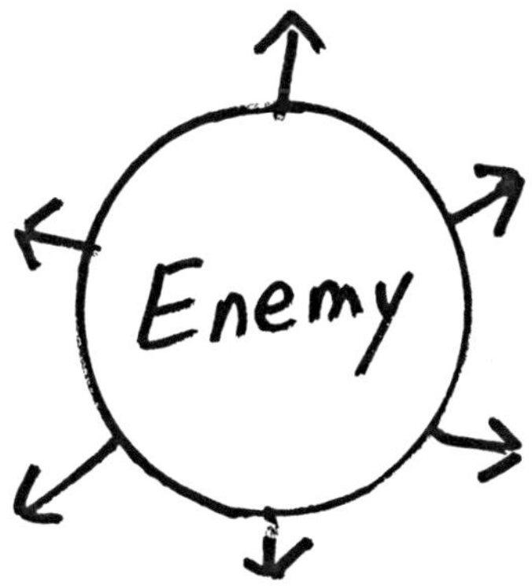
Enemy

GLOBAL DICTIONARY

There are many words in the English language which have different meanings. We can usually tell which meaning is intended or preferred by looking at the way in which that word is used in a sentence. See how many different meanings you can find for each word below. Try to find at least two meanings for each word. Then write a complete sentence to show that particular meaning of the word.

RACE:

Meanings: ______________________________

____

____

Sentences: ______________________________

____

____

UNION:

Meanings: ______________________________

____

____

Sentences: ______________________________

____

____

REVOLUTION:

Meanings: ____________________

____

____

Sentences: ____________________

____

____

CULTURE:

Meanings: ____________________

____

____

Sentences: ____________________

____

____

STRIKE:

Meanings: ____________________

____

____

Sentences: ____________________

____

____

LIBERATION:

Meanings: ______________________________

____

____

Sentences: ______________________________

____

____

CONFLICT:

Meanings: ______________________________

____

____

Sentences: ______________________________

____

____

DEMOCRATIC:

Meanings: ______________________________

____

____

Sentences: ______________________________

____

____

IMPERIALIST:

Meanings: ______________________________

____

____

Sentences: ______________________________

____

____

NATIONALISM:

Meanings: ______________________________

____

____

Sentences: ______________________________

____

____

NUCLEAR:

Meanings: ______________________________

____

____

Sentences: ______________________________

____

____

Handout #9

TERMINOLOGY OF DEVELOPMENT

Below are some terms which have been used to describe nations and regions of the world:

-- Developed World

-- Underdeveloped World

-- Developing World

-- Emerging Nations

-- Rich Nations

-- Poor Nations

-- Third World

-- Dependent Countries

-- Interdependent Countries

-- Afro-Asian Bloc (or World)

-- Western World

-- Non-Western World

-- Uncommitted Nations

-- Northern/Southern Hemisphere

-- ______________________________

-- ______________________________

-- ______________________________

-- ______________________________

-- ______________________________

-- ______________________________

-- ______________________________

-- ______________________________

-- ______________________________

-- ______________________________

-- ______________________________

-- ______________________________

-- ______________________________

MAP OF WORLD

REWRITING HISTORY

1. Nor have we been wanting in attention to our British brethren. We have warned them from time to time of attempts by their legislature to extend an unwarrantable jurisdiction over us. We have reminded them of the circumstances of our emigration and settlement here. We have appealed to their native justice and magnanimity, and we have conjured them by the ties of our common kindred to disavow these usurpations, which would inevitably interrupt our connections and correspondence. They too have been deaf to the voice of justice and of consanguinity. We must, therefore, acquiesce in the necessity, which denounces our Separation, and hold them, as we hold the rest of mankind, Enemies in War, in Peace Friends.

Thomas Jefferson, Benjamin Franklin, John Adams

- -

2. . . . a wise and frugal Government, which shall restrain men from injuring one another, shall leave them otherwise free to regulate their own pursuits of industry and improvement, and shall not take from the mouth of labor the bread it has earned. This is the sum of good government, and this is necessary to close the circle of our felicities. . .

Jefferson's Inaugural Address (1801)

3. Observe good faith and justice toward all nations. Cultivate peace and harmony with all. Religion and morality enjoin this conduct, and can it be that good policy does not equally enjoin it? It will be worthy of a free, enlightened, and, at no distant period, a great nation, to give to mankind the magnanimous and too novel example of a people always guided by an exalted justice and benevolence.

   Who can doubt that, in the course of time and things, the fruits of such a plan would richly repay any temporary advantages that might be lost by a steady adherence to it?

   Can it be, that Providence has not connected the permanent felicity of a nation with its virtue?

   The experiment, at least is recommended by every sentiment which ennobles human nature.

Washington's Farewell Address (1796)

- -

4. When in the Course of human events, it becomes necessary for one people to dissolve the political bands which have connected them with another, and to assume among the Powers of the earth, the separate and equal station to which the Laws of Nature and of Nature's God entitle them, a decent respect to the opinions of mankind requires that they should declare the causes which impel them to the separation.

The Declaration of Independence
(July 4, 1776)

SAY AGAIN, PLEASE

FORM 1*

In the event of default in the payment of this or any other Obligation or the performance or observance of any term or covenant contained herein or in any note or other contract or agreement evidencing or relating to any Obligation or any Collateral on the Borrower's part to be performed or observed; or the undersigned Borrower shall die; or any of the undersigned become insolvent or make an assignment for the benefit of creditors; or a petition shall be filed by or against any of the undersigned under any provision of the Bankruptcy Act; or any money, securities or property of the undersigned now or hereafter on deposit with or in the possession or under the control of the Bank shall be attached or become subject to distraint proceedings or any order or process of any court; or the Bank shall deem itself to be insecure, then and in any such event, the Banks shall have the right (at its option), without demand or notice of any kind, to declare all or any part of the Obligation to be immediately due and payable, whereupon such Obligations shall become and be immediately due and payable, and the Bank shall have the right to exercise all the rights and remedies available to a secured party upon default and under the Uniform Commercial Code (the "Code") in effect in New York at the time, and such other rights and remedies as may otherwise be provided by law.

- -

FORM 2*

I'll be in default:

1. If I don't pay an installment on time; or

2. If any other creditor tries by legal process to take any money of mine in your possession.

   You can then demand immediate payment of the balance of this note, minus the part of the FINANCE CHARGE which hasn't been earned, calculated as stated in the Prepayment paragraph. You will also have other legal rights, for instance, the right to repossess, sell and apply security to the payments under this note and any other debts I may then owe you.

*Flightime, September, 1978, pp. 41-43; 55.

Handout #13

TRUTH IN ADVERTISING?

Helps control dandruff with regular use. ______________________________

____

Listerine fights bad breath. ______________________________

____

Ivory liquid for younger-looking hands. ______________________________

____

Only half the price of many color sets. ______________________________

____

Genuine imitation processed cheese. ______________________________

____

You can be sure if its Westinghouse. ______________________________

____

Magnovox gives you more. ______________________________

____

Geritol has more than twice the iron of ordinary supplements. ____________

____

Winston tastes good like a cigarette should. ______________________________

____

Wonder Bread helps build strong bodies twelve ways. ______________________________

____

Strong enough for a man but made for a woman. ______________________________

____

You've come a long way, baby. ______________________________

____

We do it all for you. ______________________________

____

Tastes like the real thing. ______________________________

____

Cleaner skin in only five days. ______________________________

____

Handout #14

BUZKASHI

Buzkashi, which means "goat dragging" or "grabbing," is an exceptionally violent game that tribes in northern Afghanistan (Afghan Turkestan) play on horseback. Besides expressing the fierce and incessant social rivalry that preoccupies Afghans, buzkashi also indicates the important role that the horse has played in central Asian history. Early armies of nomadic horsemen could assemble quickly, cover great distances, attack, and at full gallop and without dismounting, sweep up women, animals, and plunder. Genghis Khan used cavalry to establish an empire that stretched from northern China to the Mediterranean. He then employed mounted couriers to transmit orders and news over his empire's routes.

Although buzkashi's historical origins are unclear, they may lie in a traditional exercise of central Asian horsemen, who trained by riding, in turn, past a ditch and attempting to pick up a beheaded goat, or buz. No one knows when its exercise became a game in which all riders simultaneously attempted to seize the goat, which is now a calf carcass.

Of the many Afghan sayings concerning horses, one is, "Better to have a poor rider on a good horse than a good rider on a poor horse," an expression of the Afghan belief that buzkashi belongs to the horse. In northern Afghanistan, the horse is the focus of complex personal tribal ambitions and rivalries. Chiefs feel that their honor is closely tied to the qualities of their horses and will spare no amount of expense and energy on feeding and exercising their animals--and on the rituals surrounding them. Horse racing, once an important form of competition, has largely been replaced by the more violent pastime of buzkashi. One Afghan explained: "Everything in buzkashi is rivalry."

The groups involved in buzkashi on the vast plain of northern Afghanistan are primarily Uzbek and Turkoman (Turkic-speaking) populations, seminomadic sheep breeders and dry farmers who migrated across the Amu Darya (ancient Oxus River) from Central Asia. Among them live large groups of Persian-speaking Tajik, who excel at irrigation farming, and more recent settlers like the Hazara, of Mongol origin, and the Pushtuns, who are either farmers of nomads.

In recent years, buzkashi games have become more frequent. At the end of the nineteenth century, during the last part of Afghanistan's feudal period, tribal chiefs faced a weak central government, and fought continually among themselves for supremacy. Since the beginning of the twentieth century, the central government has gradually grown stronger. Simultaneously, buzkashi has replaced actual warfare as the most visible manifestation of the chiefs' political ambitions.

*"Buzkashi" by Asen Balikei, with permission from NATURAL HISTORY, Vol. 87, No. 2. Copyright the American Museum of Natural History, 1978.

CARAVANS

The time had now come for disbanding the camp and I discovered that this event was traditionally marked by a game of Afghan polo. Early one morning Zulfiqar sent Maftoon to find me and the cameleer asked, "You like to play polo?"

I said, "Tell Zulfiqar I know nothing about polo," but Mira clapped her hands and cried, "Tell Zulfiqar he'll play." But when I saddled up she checked the lashing and warned, "Better tie everything twice. The game can get rough."

I joined Zulfiqar and we rode to a field east of the confluence, where children waited, chattering with excitement, and the women of the camp, who made a place for Ellen and Mira. The field was crowded with horsemen clustering about the old Hazara, who was trying to establish some ground-and-ready rules. He did not ride his horse well, for under his left arm he held a white goat who struggled to get free, but the old man did succeed in showing us the two goal lines, about two hundred yards apart. Then he cried, "Shakkur, have your men pass out the arm bands," and the big Kirghiz gave the signal.

Shakkur gave me a white arm band and said, "Fight well."

It was to be south-of-the-Oxus versus north-of-the-Oxus, for Shakkur kept on his team the Uzbeks, Tajiks, Kazaks and Kirghizes, while Zulfiqar had riders from Afghanistan, India, China and Persia. There were about forty to a side, but the reasons which became apparent to me later on, no one bothered to insure that we were evenly matched.

Zulfiqar's White team lined up to defend the eastern goal and the Russians opposed us. In the center the old Hazara held aloft the goat by his rear legs while an Uzbek whipped out a knife and cut off the animal's head. With a savage cry the umpire threw the goat's body high in the air and left the field, not to interfere again. Before the goat, spurting blood, could land, a Tajik horseman swept in, caught the animal and raised it over his head in a mad gallop toward our goal line. He had covered only a few yards when he was hit from three sides by our riders, who tackled, grabbed, gouged and beat him. Finally one of our Turkomans leaped almost clear of his horse, grabbed the goat and wrenched it away from the battered Tajik, who was now bleeding from the mouth.

Our Turkoman set off boldly for the Russian goal, but a force of shouting Uzbeks and Kirghizes slammed into him and not only stole the goat but also knocked down his horse, so that he catapulted across the rocky playing field. No one stopped to see if he was hurt, and after a while he recovered his horse and rejoined the game. Meanwhile, one of our Afghans drew even with Uzbek who had captured the goat and literally threw himself at his opponent, knocking the Russian rider right out of the saddle, but before the goat touched the earth, Shakkur the Kirghiz sped in, caught it by one leg and fought his way through the mob to find himself with a clear path to our goal. The polo game was over, for no White rider could possibly catch him.

At this point the essential feature of Afghan polo was made clear. When the victorious Russian team saw that their captain was about to score they regretted that the game was ending, so one of their own men, a fiery Uzbek, set forth in hot pursuit and just as the baldheaded sharif was about to cross our line, this Uzbek teammate came up from behind, gave him a wallop across the back of his neck, grabbed the goat and brought it back into play. Both sides applauded, and the game continued. Thereafter, when some player threatened to score, his own teammates slugged him, gouged him and tried to knock him from his horse. It was always one rider fighting forty of the enemy plus thirty-nine of his friends, and sometimes it was the latter who did the worst damage.

For nearly sixty bruising minutes we played without my distinguishing myself--it seemed that half the other riders were bleeding from the mouth--when I happened to gallop past the children of our caravan and heard them shout, "Get in the game." I saw Ellen, and she looked a bit stunned by the brutality of the sport, but little Mira was furious. "Why did I get you the horse?" she shouted. "Do something!"

So I dashed into the middle of the fracas, where I accomplished nothing until a north-of-the-Oxus Kazak broke loose with what was left of the goat and headed in my general direction. It was apparent that unless I stopped him, the game was over, so I tried to turn him back into the mob, but the Russian decided that he could scare me into yielding ground, so he drive directly at me, and so far as I was concerned this strategy would have worked, for I was willing to withdraw, but Moheb´s horse had been trained for just his kind of challenge and, ignoring my reins, leaped ahead seeking contact. We struck the Kazak with stunning force, spun him around and caused him to drop the goat, which to my surprise I caught.

But before I got started for the Russian goal, I caught a glimpse of Shakkur bearing down on me and in order to escape him tried evasive action. He anticipated my move and with his left arm clubbed me across the back so violently that I nearly pitched over my horse´s head. In attempting to regain control I exposed the goat, which Shakkur grabbed, literally tearing it from me. He rode off with the body; I was left with one leg.

Dazed from his blow, I started in pursuit, but the chase was fruitless, for Shakkur had a clear run for the goal, and even though one of his own Kazaks tried to knock him from his horse, the big sharif defended himself by clubbing the Kazak in the face with the bloody goat. Thus ended our game of polo, the sport of gentlemen.

PROVERBS

1. Chickens always come home to roost. (Alabama)
2. Ice three feet thick isn´t frozen in a day. (China)
3. Young gambler - old beggar. (Germany)
4. Where the river is deepest it makes the least noise. (Italy)
5. If you climb up a tree, you must climb down that same tree. (Ghana)
6. You cannot get two skins from one cow. (England)
7. Eggs must not quarrel with stones. (China)
8. A horse that arrives early gets good drinking water. (Africa)
9. The love of money is the root of all evil. (Israel)
10. Words thoughtlessly said cannot be called back. (Louisiana)
11. The wife at another´s house has the pretty eyes. (Africa)
12. God gives the milk but not the pail. (Germany)
13. Pinch yourself to know how painful it is to others. (Japan)
14. A bird in the hand is worth a hundred flying. (Mexico)
15. Sing and cares disappear. (Poland)
16. One man´s story is no story; hear both sides. (Japan)
17. God is a good worker, but he loves to be helped. (Spain)
18. Many a good man is to be found under a shabby hat. (China)
19. Fine clothes don´t make the man. (Japan)
20. By trying often, the monkey learns to jump from the tree. (Zaire)
21. You can force a man to shut his eyes, but you can´t make him sleep. (Denmark)
22. Two captains sink the ship. (Japan)
23. Little by little grow the bananas. (Dahomey)
24. If you want to go fast, go the old road. (Burma)
25. Six feet of earth makes all men equal. (Italy)
26. Eat to live, not live to eat. (Greece)
27. He who stand with his feet on two ships will be drowned. (USSR)
28. A little in your own pocket is better than much in another´s purse. (Spain)

29. Joy, moderation, and rest shut out the doctors. (Germany)

30. He who rides the tiger finds it difficult to dismount. (China)

31. It is when one is in trouble that he remembers God. (Africa)

32. A kind word will help build a house, a bitter one will destroy it. (Armenia)

33. He who sleeps with children wakes up sopping wet. (New Mexico)

34. Women hold up half the sky. (China)

35. The rain does not all fall on one roof. (Africa)

IT MAKES THE WORLD GO ROUND

A Conversation on Marriage

Heather: I just find it hard to believe that in India you want your parents to arrange your marriage, Radhika.

Radhika: Well, Heather, it seems strange to me that American girls should want to find their own husbands.

Heather: Does it really? I still can't believe it.

Radhika: Well, don't you find it humiliating to have to attract boys?

Heather: What do you mean?

Radhika: Let me try to explain. As I understand your system in the United States, getting married depends on whether a girl can attract a boyfriend. She must call attention to herself, using makeup, hair styles, and the latest clothing fashions to make herself look pretty. If she is shy, and doesn't want to do all that, she might end up unmarried.

Heather: Well, don't some women remain unmarried in India?

Radhika: Under arranged marriage, we don't have to worry about that. We know we'll be married. When we reach the proper age, our parents will find a suitable boy. We don't have to compete with other girls. We don't have to pretend we're better than we are in order to attract a boy. We can simply be ourselves. Trying to make a good impression on boys must truly be humiliating.

Heather: But how can you marry someone if you're not in love with him?

Radhika: We realize that love can blind us. It can make us ignore problems that will give us much trouble later on. Our parents are older and wiser. They are better able to choose the right boy. I could easily make a mistake because I am so young.

But don't think there is no love in arranged marriage. We expect to fall in love with our husbands, and that's what usually happens. An Indian poetess in the thirteenth century explained the way we view our future husband:

Howard Mellinger, et al., Global Studies for American Schools, published by National Education Association

Without seeing thy face I have given thee a place
in my own eye, like the pupil.
I have only heard thy name and I love thee.
I have not seen thee, and yet I love thee as if I
had seen and known thee.

Heather: But surely, this doesn´t always work out. Don´t some arranged marriages end in divorce?

Radhika: Well, yes, divorce sometimes occurs. More often, though, if the match is not a good one, people just put up with an unhappy marriage. If the family is poor, they might have no other choice.

But surely unhappy marriage is a bigger problem in the United States. I have read that one out of every three marriages ends in divorce in your country. Many seem to fall "out of love," don´t they?

Heather: You´re right that divorce affects many people in the U.S. And I can see better now why you like arranged marriages. But there is one thing Americans insist on that you do not have in arranged marriage --individual choice. We do not rely on our parents to choose a husband for us. Our parents, after all, won´t have to live with him, but we will. We want to make our own choice, our own decision. Even if it turns out to be an unhappy marriage, we don´t wish to give up our right to choose.

Radhika: I see. Our different ways of choosing a marriage partner certainly show up interesting differences between our cultures.

Questions

1. What "interesting differences" between India and the United States can you see in this conversation? First, list what was important to Radhika in finding a husband. Next, list what was important to Heather. Then compare.

2. Compare Radhika´s view of parents with your view of parents.

3. How would you answer Radhika´s comment that it must be humiliating for girls to try to impress boys? Would she say the same about boys trying to impress girls? Are "looking just right" and "making good impressions" big worries of American teenagers?

4. What commercials would not be on television if the U.S. practiced arranged marriages?

USES FOR THE NEWSPAPER

1. Creativity: Roll up a piece of newspaper and tape it. What could it be? Pantomime your ideas for the class.
2. Creative Writing: Take a comic strip out of the newspaper. Cover up the words and insert your own captions.
3. Take a newspaper and find and circle or underline all the parts of speech you can.
4. Take a newspaper, and cut out a word or words. Make this the basis of a collage or a new article.
5. In groups of two or three people, write a short story using words cut out of a newspaper.
6. Use newspaper to make a papier mache art object, such as an animal. Paint it.
7. Cut out pictures from the newspaper and make up stories about them.
8. Make a bulletin board entitled "In the News." Bring in articles, share them with the class, and put them on the bulletin board.
9. List ten countries or states mentioned in the first ten pages of the newspaper. What is happening in those places? Who is involved?
10. Make a chart of the win-loss record for the hometown teams for different sports by following the sports section of the newspaper.
11. Find your spelling words in the newspaper.
12. Dictionary Activity: Find unfamiliar words in the newspaper; look them up in a dictionary and write down the meaning.
13. Summarize a particular newspaper article in two or three sentences.
14. Use newspaper as a background for a painting.
15. See how many ways you can make a paper airplane by folding a newspaper in different ways.

Developed by Katherine J. Holderith

NEWS ITEMS

A. Earthquake strikes in Central America; causes over 500 deaths and leaves thousands homeless.

B. New kind of high-yield wheat developed which may help solve world food shortage.

C. Saudi Arabian businessmen buy controlling interest in United States film company.

D. Development and production of electric cars as a source of pollution-free transportation announced.

E. Friends say that actor Paul Newman may go into politics, possibly running for Congress if he can develop enough support.

F. State court in New Jersey tells chemical company that it must stop dumping wastes in town's water supply.

G. Government issues warning on canned tuna fish distributed by Star of the Sea Canning Company; some cans have been contaminated and may cause severe illness.

H. National weather service predicts extremely cold winter this year.

I. British astronomer reports that a radio telescope has picked up signals from deep space that could be some form of intelligent communication.

J. The first successful human cloning is announced in Cambridge, Mass.

K. The long-standing border dispute between Vietnam and Kampuchea may be almost settled; negotiators report that an agreement will be signed soon.

L. Three members of the Italian terrorist group, the Red Brigade, responsible for the assassination of numerous government officials, were sentenced to life imprisonment in Rome today.

M. The annual population growth rate has begun to rise again in India after reaching an all-time low of 2 percent last year.

N. High school student sets new mark in Guiness Book of World Records by swallowing forty-three goldfish.

O. A day in the life of a worker on the Alaskan pipeline. (feature story)

P. Soybeans--a valuable source of protein for the world. (feature story)

Q. Cuban baseball team offers challenge to U.S. club to play series to determine true world champion. (feature story)

R. A report on increasing use of robots as household servants and office aides. (feature story)

EDITORIAL

The city-wide strike of firemen and policemen is now entering its second week. At issue are the terms of the new contract for these city employees. Policemen and firemen walked off their jobs when negotiations with the city broke down. Since then, skeleton crews have been operating throughout the city. However, loss of property is rising. Arson has been reported in several parts of the city, and looting is becoming a problem in the business district. The mayor has said that the money for increased wages is simply unavailable and the union has vowed not to resume police and fire protection until wage demands have been met. Both sides are resisting arbitration.

Handout #21

TV STATIONS

TV Station A

You hope to attract audiences by appealing to sensationalism, complete with dramatic pictures, reporting, and grim statistics.

TV Station B

You hope to attract audiences by focusing on controversial issues and conflict between different groups.

TV Station C

You hope to attract audiences by entertaining them; you try to use humor whenever possible.

TV Station D

You hope to attract audiences by the use of human interest stories, focusing on the lives and activities of ordinary people.

TV Station E

You hope to attract audiences by criticizing the inefficiency and corruption of government and elected officials.

TV Station F

You hope to attract audiences by providing useful and practical information that will help people solve real-life problems.

ON YOUR OWN

1. Write an article about the Arab-Israeli conflict in the Middle East from an Israeli, Iraqi, or Palestinian point of view.

2. Compare the Middle East conflict with violence in Northern Ireland or with the India-Pakistan war.

3. Summarize the history of the Middle East region in the twentieth century.

4. Write a human interest story in the form of a magazine article or newspaper report about a Jew in Israel, an Iraqi, or a Palestinian terrorist.

5. Write a commercial for a documentary film dealing with the Arab-Israeli conflict.

6. Write a diplomatic dispatch on the results of a summit meeting between Israel and Iraq.

7. Compare the history of Israel and Iraq.

8. Interview an Israeli soldier and an Iraqi; a member of a kibbutz; a displaced Palestinian; a Lebanese Christian, a Saudi Arabian oil minister, or a member of the PLO.

9. Write a poem about some aspect of the Arab-Israeli conflict.

10. Compare the Jewish and Moslem religions using the Bible and the Koran as sources.

11. Write an on-the-spot radio or TV broadcast of an event related to the conflict (e.g., the 1967 or 1973 War, the PLO, terrorist bombing in Jerusalem, the closing of the Suez Canal).

12. Do a report on an author or poet who has written on life in the Middle East.

13. Trace the events leading to the establishment of the Arab League, or the state of Israel in 1984.

14. Write an article about race and ethnicity from a scientist's or an anthropologist's point of view.

15. Compare the treatment of Jews in different cultures (e.g., Germany, USSR, U.S.).

16. Defend the concept of a Palestinian homeland; argue against it.

17. Write a research paper on some aspect of the Arab-Israeli conflict (historical, cultural, political, comparative, religious, criticism).

18. Rate Israel and the Arab states (Egypt, Saudi Arabia, Jordan, Syria, Iraq) on their commitment to human rights.

GLOBAL HEADLINES

____

____

New York - Scientific discoveries sometimes hinge on luck, and the remarkable drama witnessed by the Rockefeller University's Dr. Donald Griffin took place during the final hour of a two-day visit the distinguished biologist paid to Kenya's Amboseli National Park in 1980.

Griffin wasn't working--"I was just a tourist visiting friends," he said--but while observing a large herd of wildebeests grazing peacefully, Griffin noticed four lionesses approaching. The predators' gait was 'businesslike,' he said.

The wildebeests stopped feeding and watched intently.

About 200 yards from the herd, two of the lionesses climbed slowly atop adjoining earthen mounds. "They sat down and remained stationary," Griffin said, "but conspicuous."

The wildebeests stared at the pair. When no threat was forthcoming, they resumed grazing.

Then, Griffin spotted a third lioness, unnoticed, slinking on her belly through a ditch in front of the herd.

"She soon crawled out of our view, and for several minutes, nothing seemed to be happening at all."

Suddenly, a fourth lioness appeared behind the herd.

She charged, sending the panicked wildebeests thundering directly toward the lioness in the ditch.

As about 50 of the wildebeests bounded over her, she leapt up, seized one, and killed it. The other lionesses then walked over in what Griffin describes as "a very leisurely fashion" and settled down for dinner.

How to explain what Griffin saw?

It could have all been coincidental, he admitted. The event also could be explained as a triumph of evolution and natural selection. The lionesses may merely have been following the behavioral instructions of their genetic heritage refined by techniques they had learned from hunting wildebeests.

To Griffin, though, the answer may be even more provocative: Perhaps he observed a calculated diversion and ambush conducted by a team of communicating lionesses; an ingenious plot requiring, among other things, intelligence, foresight, meticulous timing and crisp execution.

In other words, the cats may have been thinking about what they were doing.

"There's no way to prove it, at least not yet," Griffin said. "But I think the possibility exists."

* *

____

____

BEIRUT, Lebanon - A van driven by a suicide bomber careened past concrete barriers and through a fusillade of gunfire Thursday, blowing up at the doors of the U.S. Embassy annex. Police said 23 people were killed in the blast, and the Pentagon reported two of the dead were Americans.

Lebanese state radio initially put the death toll at 10, but later said as many as 40 people may have perished.

The blast tore into the lower stories of the six-story building, injuring as many as 60 people, including the British and American ambassadors and 21 other Americans, police and emergency officials said.

* *

____

____

CAIRO, Egypt -- The multinational search for mines in the Red Sea moved back into high gear Friday after an explosion that damaged a Saudi ship and the discovery of devices believed to be mines.

The French, who had planned to break off their search Thursday, instead extended it, perhaps for as long as a week. And the Italians sent their mine-hunters into the Gulf of Suez at Egypt's request.

The explosion Thursday involving the Saudi Arabian passenger vessel Belkis was the first reported in the Red Sea or Gulf of Suez since August 15. It brought the number of ships damaged by underwater explosions to 19 since July 9.

____

____

More than 100 giant pandas have died in the past 4 years, but their killers are neither hunters nor pollution. The creatures are starving. Their main source of food is the umbrella bamboo, which flowers and drops its seed once a century, then the plant dies. The pandas have little food until the new plants grow.

Chinese and American scientists have gone to the Chinese highlands to see how they might help the 1000 surviving animals. The scientists hope to learn how the pandas have adapted to the loss of bamboo. They also plan to watch the pandas' living habits.

* *

____

____

When a teen-age boy takes the family car and leaves home for the night, it's not normally front-page news. But when the 16-year-old son of an important Soviet diplomat in Washington did just that last week--and wrote a letter to The New York Times--it became an international incident. The letter, signed by Andrei V. Berezhkov, son of the Soviet Embassy's first secretary, Valentin M. Berezhkov, explained: "I hate my country and it's [sic] rules and I love your country. I want to stay here. . ."

The Soviet Embassy called the letter a forgery and a "very clear provocation to us." The U.S. State Department said it wanted to speak directly with the boy. At the weekend, it received assurances that young Andrei was still in the country--despite some reports that he was on a plane to Moscow.

* *

____

____

When the British Transglobe expedition set off almost three years ago it sounded like just the sort of plucky stunt that only a crazed canine or Englishman would ever attempt. "Mad but marvelous," declared Prince Charles, as explorers Charles Burton and Sir Ranulph Fiennes left England in 1979, determined to be the first to circle the earth from pole to pole. They reached their first major objective, the South Pole, sixteen months ago. Last week they reached their second, planting the Union Jack at the North Pole four days ahead of schedule--and overnight the two explorers became national heroes.

*

____

____

"All I remember was loud noise and then it started coming down," said construction worker Robert Gilbert. "People started to holler and I ran." As workers poured concrete high atop an unfinished highway bridge in East Chicago, Ind., last week, three sections of the bridge suddenly collapsed, sending men and debris crashing down 60 feet and crushing other workers below. At least twelve men were killed and seventeen were injured; rescue workers found one man lodged head first in a hardened concrete pillar. Authorities initially feared that many more had been pinned under the twisted mass of steel and concrete.

Officials said it would be weeks before the cause of the collapse was known. But some experts surmised that one section of the scaffolding failed to support the weight of the concrete, and that stress and vibrations from the first collapse caused the other sections to buckle. Meanwhile, some parts of the bridge hung by threads of steel cable and workers posted a guard at the site to prevent others from being injured.

Handout #24

HUMAN RIGHTS POSTERS

Scenario 1:

Argentina has been accused of persistent violations of human rights. Your group is concerned with the plight of political prisoners in Argentina, people detained in prisons because of their political views. Amnesty International said there are thousands of such prisoners. You also deplore tactics such as torture used in these prisons. You want to make the public and especially the government aware of this situation.

Scenario 2:

Argentina has been accused of persistent violations of human rights. Your group is opposed to U.S. economic and military aid to Argentina as long as these violations continue to occur. You especially want to make your view known to the U.S. Congress which has the power to grant or deny that aid to Argentina.

Scenario 3:

Argentina has been accused of persistent violations of human rights. Your group is opposed to military dictatorships as a form of government and sees the human rights situation in Argentina as an outgrowth of this repressive form of government. You want to make the public aware of the nature of these violations and use this as another reason for advocating a change in government and return to more democratic rule.

Scenario 4:

Argentina has been accused of persistent violations of human rights. Your group is committed to the cause of human rights around the world but takes a moderate stand in bringing about change. You take the positive approach of publicizing a country's achievements in human rights, no matter how small. Thus, you wish to gain more concessions in the field of human rights by accentuating what you see as positive steps and de-emphasizing blatant violations.

PROTEST POETRY

WHAT WERE THEY LIKE? (Questions and Answers) by Denise Levertov

1. Did the people of Vietnam use lanterns of stone?
2. Did they hold ceremonies to reverence the opening of buds?
3. Were they inclined to rippling laughter?
4. Did they use bone and ivory, jade and silver, for ornament?
5. Had they an epic poem?
6. Did they distinguish between speech and singing?

1. Sir, their light hearts turned to stone.
   It is not remembered whether in gardens
   stone lanterns illuminated pleasant ways.

2. Perhaps they gathered once to delight in blossom,
   but after the children were killed there were no more buds.

3. Sir, laughter is bitter to the burned mouth.

4. A dream ago, perhaps. Ornament is for joy.
   All the bones were charred.

5. It is not remembered. Remember, most were peasants;
   their life was in rice and bamboo.
   When peaceful clouds were reflected in the paddies
   and the water-buffalo stepped surely along terraces,
   maybe fathers told their sons old tales.
   When bombs smashed the mirrors there was time only to scream.

6. There is an echo yet, it is said,
   of their speech which was like a song.
   It is reported their singing resembled
   the flight of moths in moonlight.
   Who can say? It is silent now.

CHILE STADIUM

Victor Jara

There are five thousand of us here
in this little part of the city.
We are five thousand.
I wonder how many we are in all
in the cities and in the whole country?
Here alone
are ten thousand hands which plant seeds
and make the factories run.
How much humanity
exposed to hunger, cold, panic, pain
moral pressures, terror and insanity?
Six of us were lost
as if into starry space.
One dead, another beaten as I could never have believed
a human being could be beaten.
The other four wanted to end their terror--
one jumping into nothingness,
another beating his head against a wall,
but all with the fixed look of death.
What horror the fact of fascism creates!
They carry out their plans with knife-like precision.
Nothing matters to them
For them blood equals medals,
slaughter is an act of heroism.
Oh God, is this the world that you created?
For this, your seven days of wonder and work?
Within these four walls only a number exists
which does not progress.
Which slowly will wish more and more for death.
But suddenly my conscience awakes
and I see this tide with no heartbeat,
only the pulse of machines
and the military showing their midwives faces
full of sweetness.
Let Mexico, Cuba and world
cry out against this atrocity!
We are ten thousand hands
which can produce nothing
How many of us in the whole country?
The blood of our companero Presidente
will strike with more strength than bombs and machine guns!

Walter Lowenfels, ed., For Neruda, For Chile, An International Anthology, Boston: Beacon Press, 1975.

How hard it is to sing
When I must sing of horror.
Horror which I am living

Horror which I am dying.
To see myself among so much
and so many moments of infinity
in which silence and screams
are the end of my song.
What I see I have never seen
What I have felt and what I feel
will give birth to the moment...

Translated from the Spanish by
Joan Jara

NICE DAY FOR A LYNCHING

by Kenneth Patchen

The bloodhounds look like sad old judges
In a strange court. They point their noses
At the Negro jerking in the tight noose;
His feet spread crow-like above these
Honorable men who laugh as he chokes.

I don´t know this black man.
I don´t know these white men.

Kenneth Patchen, Collected Poems. New York: New Directions, 1968.

by e. e. cummings

"next to of course god america i
love you land of the pilgrims' and so forth oh
say can you see by the dawn's early my
country 'tis of centuries come and go
and are no more what of it we should worry
in every language even deaf and dumb
thy sons acclaim your glorious name by gorry
by lingo by gee by gosh by gum
why talk of beauty what could be more beautiful than these
heroic happy dead
who rushed like lions to the roaring slaughter
they did not stop to think they died instead
then should the voice of liberty be mute?"

He spoke. And drank rapidly a glass of water

E. E. Cummings, Complete Poems of E. E. Cummings 1913-1962. New York: Harcourt Brace, 1968.

AT HIROSHIMA

When we came out of the station
The houses looked old, and we wondered.

But after we had walked for a while
We came to a place with wide streets

And all the buildings were new.
Children were playing on the sidewalks,

Crying to each other in shrill voices.
Bicycles went by, jingling their bells.

But we knew we were standing
Where the end of the world began.

Lindley Williams Hubbell, Seventy Poems. Swallow Press, 1965.

I, TOO, SING AMERICA

I, too, sing America.

I am the darker brother.
They send me to eat in the kitchen
When company comes,
But I laugh,
And eat well,
And grow strong.

Tomorrow,
I'll be at the table
When company comes.
Nobody'll dare
Say to me,
"Eat in the kitchen,"

Then.
Besides,
They'll see how beautiful I am.
And be ashamed--

I, too, am America.

Langston Hughes, Selected Poems. NY: Alfred A. Knopf, 1959.

Printed in the United States
106176LV00001B/398/A

Édité par Hachette Livre – 58, rue Jean Bleuzen – 92178 Vanves Cedex
Imprimé par Estella Graficas en Espagne – Achevé d'imprimer : novembre 2019
ISBN : 978-2-01-707336-9 – Édition : 02 – Dépôt légal : janvier 2019
Loi n°49-956 du 16 juillet 1949 sur les publications destinées à la jeunesse.

Pour tout renseignement concernant nos parutions, nous contacter
par téléphone au 01 43 92 38 88 ou par e-mail : disney@hachette-livre.fr

Pour l'éditeur, le principe est d'utiliser des papiers composés de fibres naturelles, renouvelables, recyclables et fabriquées à partir de bois issus de forêts qui adoptent un système d'aménagement durable. En outre, l'éditeur attend de ses fournisseurs de papier qu'ils s'inscrivent dans une démarche de certification environnementale reconnue.

Disney

Peter Pan

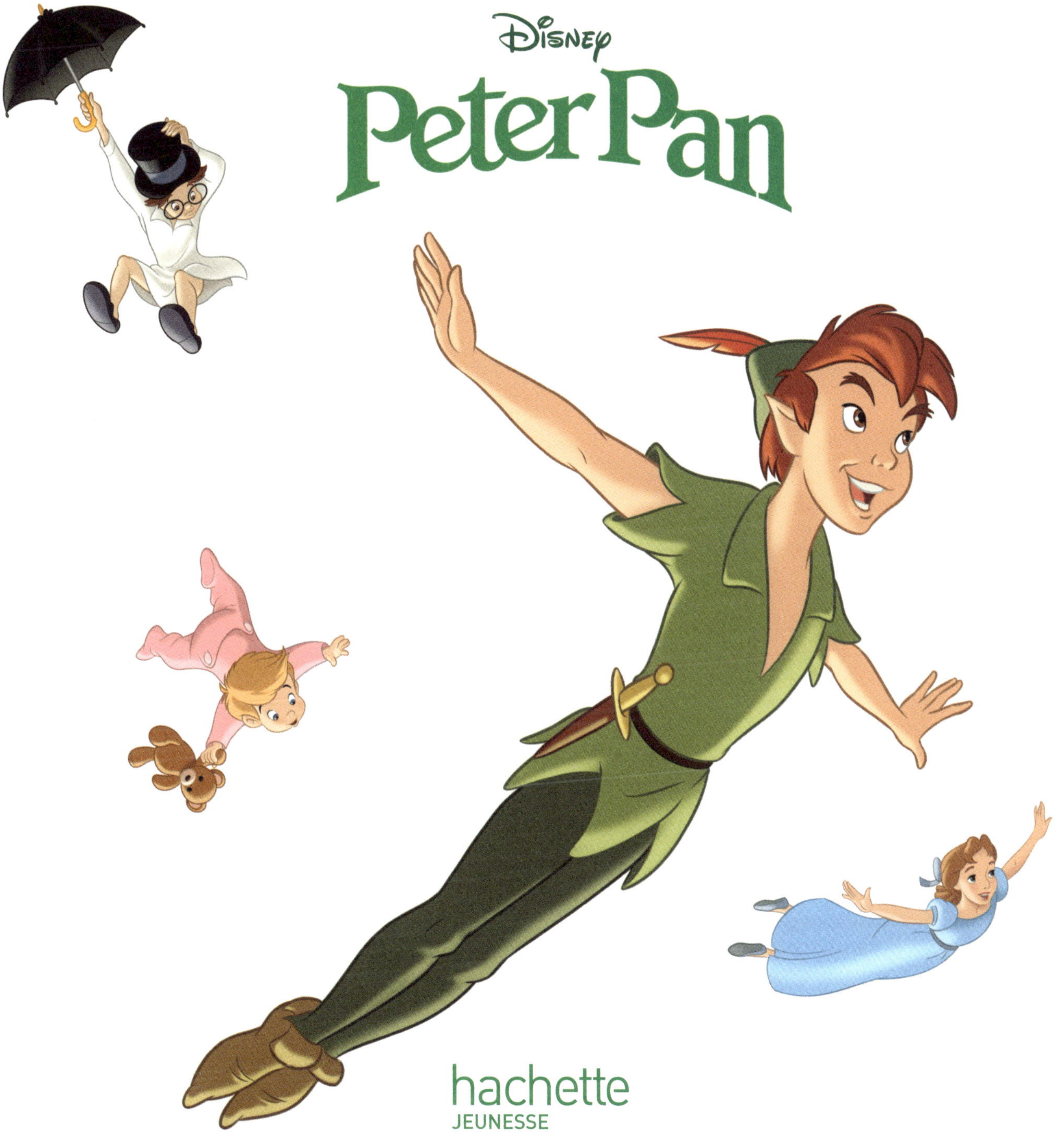

hachette
JEUNESSE

À Londres, dans leur chambre, Jean et Michel Darling font semblant de se battre.
« **Tu as perdu, Peter Pan!** s'écrie Jean.
– Sûrement pas ! Rends-toi, Capitaine Crochet », rétorque Michel, son petit frère.

Les deux garçons adorent mimer les exploits de Peter Pan, leur héros préféré. Chaque soir, Wendy, leur sœur aînée, raconte une de ses aventures avant que leur nourrice, la chienne Nana, les mette au lit.

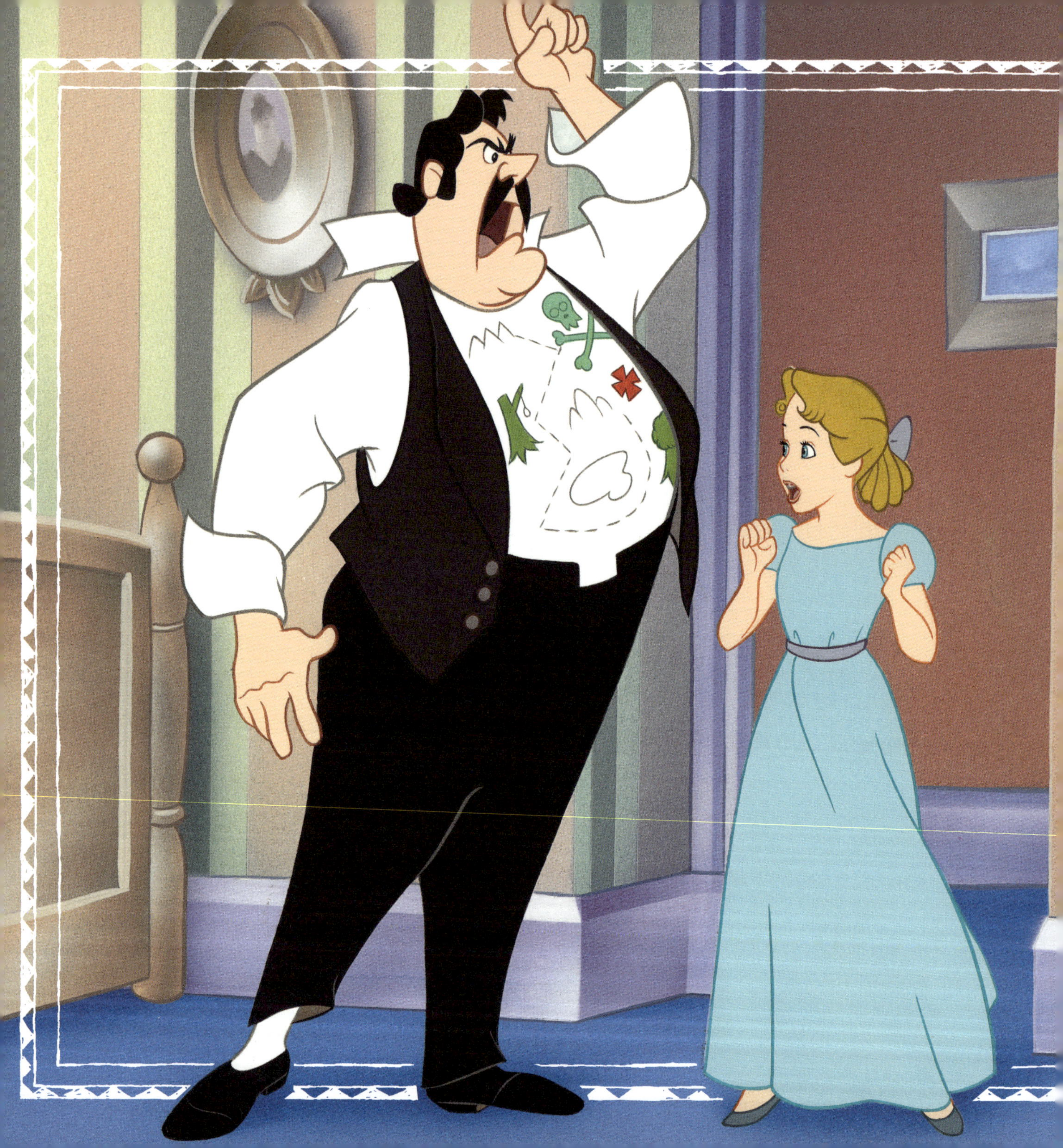

M. Darling fait irruption dans la chambre. Il a découvert son plastron décoré d'une carte au trésor et pique une colère :

« Wendy ! Je croyais t'avoir interdit de raconter ces histoires ridicules à tes frères. Ce Peter Crochet et ce Capitaine Pan…

– Peter Pan et Capitaine Crochet, Papa !

– Peu importe ! tempête M. Darling. **De toute façon, tu es grande à présent.** Tu as passé l'âge de dormir dans la chambre des enfants.

M. et Mme Darling sont sortis dîner en ville. Et les enfants dorment à poings fermés. Peter Pan et la Fée Clochette, son amie qui le suit partout, en profitent pour s'introduire dans la chambre.

Peter vient souvent écouter les histoires de Wendy, caché derrière la fenêtre.

Lors d'une récente visite, la chienne l'a surpris et lui a dérobé son ombre.
Ce soir, il revient la chercher.

« Tu es exactement comme je t'avais imaginé », murmure Wendy, réveillée par le bruit.

« Je suis bien contente que tu sois là ! confie Wendy en recousant l'ombre afin qu'elle ne s'échappe pas de nouveau. Papa vient de me gronder : il ne veut plus que je raconte des histoires aux garçons. Et je suis trop grande pour dormir dans leur chambre.

– Ah non, alors ! **Je t'emmène au Pays Imaginaire, là où l'on ne grandit jamais** », réplique Peter.

Jean et Michel se réveillent à leur tour.
« **Peter Pan nous invite au Pays Imaginaire!**
annonce Wendy.
– Chouette ! Je pars combattre des pirates ! » déclare Michel.

Peter attrape la Fée Clochette entre ses doigts.
Il la secoue au-dessus des enfants et une pluie de paillettes étincelantes les recouvre.
« Vous être prêts ? En route !... »
Peter Pan sort par la fenêtre, suivi par Wendy et ses frères.
« **C'est incroyable, on vole!** » s'émerveillent les enfants.

Ils planent au-dessus de Londres, passent **à côté de la fameuse horloge Big Ben...**

« À la deuxième étoile, on tourne à droite, et tout droit. On arrivera au petit matin ! » dit joyeusement Peter.

Quand ils arrivent en vue de l'île, le soleil se lève.
« Tout est exactement comme je l'avais rêvé, dit Wendy.
Regardez là-bas la lagune aux Sirènes !
– Et la réserve des Indiens, enchaîne Jean.
– **Le Capitaine Crochet et les pirates !** continue Michel.
– Soyez les bienvenus ! » conclut Peter Pan.

À bord de son bateau, le Capitaine Crochet cherche à repérer sur une carte la cachette de Peter Pan.

Mais un tic-tac familier détourne son attention.

« Au secours ! glapit-il. C'est encore ce crocodile ! »

Un jour, Peter Pan a coupé la main gauche du Capitaine
et l'a donnée à manger au crocodile. Depuis ce temps-là,
l'animal vient souvent rôder près du navire
et annonce sa venue par le son d'un réveil qu'il a avalé.

« **Peter Pan en vue !** » braille soudain un pirate.
Le Capitaine Crochet se précipite vers sa longue-vue.
« C'est bien lui ! Et il nous amène encore
une bande de garnements. **Tout le monde à son poste.** »

Peter Pan ordonne à Clochette d'emmener les enfants dans leur cachette, pendant qu'il s'occupe de Crochet. « **Attends-nous ! Clochette !** » l'implore Wendy qui n'arrive pas à la suivre.

Mais la Fée accélère l'allure. Elle n'aime pas du tout la tournure que prennent les événements. Que vient faire ici cette jeune fille ? En tout cas, elle ne la laissera pas prendre sa place dans le cœur de son ami. Elle sème les enfants et demande aux Garçons Perdus de les attaquer.

Heureusement, Peter arrive juste à temps.

« Qu'est-ce qui se passe ici ? tonne-t-il.
– Clochette…, bafouille l'un des Garçons Perdus, nous a demandé d'attaquer une certaine Wendy, sur ton ordre.
– Clochette ! crie Peter. **Tu es coupable de haute trahison et je te bannis à tout jamais de l'île.** »

Dépitée, la fée prend son envol.

« Suis-moi, Wendy. Je t'emmène visiter le Pays Imaginaire, s'écrie Peter. Quant à vous, les amis, allez donc capturer quelques Indiens. Toi, Jean, tu seras le chef.

– **Youpi ! On va voir des Indiens !** » s'enthousiasme Michel.

Et la troupe part en chantant.

Mais les Indiens sont les plus rapides : ils s'emparent des enfants et les conduisent à leur campement.

Le chef des Indiens s'approche et déclare dans son charabia :
« **Princesse Lili la Tigresse avoir disparu.**
Si elle pas revenue avant coucher soleil, vous être rôtis ! »

Pendant ce temps, Peter et Wendy se promènent sur l'île. Tout à coup, ils entendent des voix.

« C'est Crochet ! chuchote Peter. **Et il a enlevé Lili la Tigresse !** »

Ils se posent sur un rocher pour observer la scène qui se déroule en contrebas. Le Capitaine Crochet a ligoté la jeune Indienne et lui propose un marché.

« **Chère Princesse, si vous me dites où se trouve le repaire de Peter Pan, je vous libère sur-le-champ.** Vous feriez mieux de parler car la marée monte… »

« Le monstre ! » murmure Peter qui l'observe attentivement.

La Princesse redresse la tête et, sans un mot, affronte fièrement le regard du Capitaine.

« Pauvre Lili la Tigresse ! Peter, je t'en prie, implore Wendy. **Sauve-la !** »

« Hé, Capitaine ! crie Peter Pan d'un ton ironique.
Tu es un poisson pourri ! »

Furieux, le Capitaine dégaine son épée et se rue sur le jeune garçon.

« Allez, Capitaine ! Un petit effort !

– Tu peux faire tes prières, Peter Pan ! » conseille Crochet, sans remarquer que Peter l'entraîne vers le vide…

Et le malheureux tombe. Mouche rame à toute vitesse…
et réussit à récupérer son Capitaine,
avant que le crocodile s'en saisisse.

« Poisson pourri ! se moque de nouveau Peter Pan.

– Peter ! s'égosille Wendy. **N'oublie pas Lili la Tigresse !** »

En un clin d'œil, Peter Pan rejoint Lili.
Il défait ses liens et la soulève dans ses bras.

« **Je te ramène chez ton père !** » déclare-t-il joyeusement.

Dès leur arrivée, le chef des Indiens libère
les enfants et accueille le sauveur de sa fille.

« Toi, recevoir titre honorifique : "Petite Oie Volante" »
proclame-t-il en lui offrant une majestueuse parure de plumes.

Une grande fête est alors organisée.

Non loin de là, la Fée Clochette observe la fête en boudant quand, tout à coup, elle se sent prisonnière :

Mouche vient de l'attraper avec son bonnet.

« Désolé, mademoiselle Clochette. Ce sont les ordres du Capitaine Crochet. Il aimerait avoir une petite discussion avec vous… »

« Si seulement je savais où demeure Peter, susurre Crochet, je pourrais faire Wendy prisonnière… Bien sûr, je ne toucherai notre ami ni du doigt ni du crochet. »

La Fée lui indique aussitôt la cachette sur la carte. Alors, le Capitaine attrape Clochette, l'enferme dans une lampe en verre, puis prépare ses hommes à l'attaque.

Pendant ce temps, Wendy couche les enfants.
« Dors vite Michel : demain matin, nous rentrons à la maison.
Maman nous attend…
– C'est quoi une maman ? demande l'un des Garçons Perdus.
– **Les mamans sont les personnes**
les plus merveilleuses du monde… »
explique Wendy.

« Je veux rentrer tout de suite à la maison ! gémit Michel.
– **On vient avec vous !** » déclarent les Garçons Perdus.

Wendy hésite et finit par accepter. La petite troupe se met en marche. Peter Pan, lui, est furieux :
« C'est ça, allez-y ! Mais quand vous aurez grandi, se fâche-t-il, **jamais plus vous ne pourrez revenir ici !** »

Wendy sort à son tour du repaire.
Quelle horreur ! Tous les enfants sont ligotés et bâillonnés.

« Le compte y est ! affirme Mouche.
– Conduisez-les au bateau, ordonne le Capitaine. Je m'occupe de Peter Pan. »

« Et maintenant, mes petits agneaux, se moque Crochet, vous choisissez : vous signez et rejoignez mon équipage ou vous passez par-dessus bord. Quant à vous ma chère Wendy, sachez que nous avons laissé à Peter Pan un petit souvenir de votre part… une bombe à retardement. **À six heures pile, boum !** »

Enfermée dans sa prison de verre, Clochette entend les terribles paroles du Capitaine. Au désespoir, elle se lance de toutes ses forces contre les parois de la lampe. Celle-ci bascule et tombe, la vitre se brise et Clochette s'échappe.

Désormais, il ne lui reste que quelques minutes pour sauver Peter.

Dans sa tanière, Peter s'impatiente. Il a découvert le paquet accompagné d'un message :

Pour Peter, de la part de Wendy.
Ne pas ouvrir avant six heures !

Il meurt d'envie de savoir ce qu'il y a dedans. La pendule indique presque six heures. N'y tenant plus, il se décide à déballer son cadeau. **Clochette surgit alors et lui arrache le paquet des mains.**
« Hé ! Clochette ! Arrête ! Qu'est-ce… ? »
Boum !

Sur le bateau, les enfants refusent l'offre de Crochet.

Wendy s'avance courageusement sur la planche…
« Adieu, Jean ! Adieu, Michel ! »
Et elle se jette dans le vide. Les yeux embués de larmes,
ses deux frères retiennent leur respiration.

Curieusement, aucun bruit de chute ne suit ce plongeon !
« C'est de la sorcellerie ! » marmonne l'un des pirates.
Sous la planche, Wendy se trouve en sécurité dans les bras de Peter.

« Nous te croyions tous mort ! dit-elle, surprise de le voir là.
– Clochette est arrivée à temps, elle m'a sauvé la vie…
C'est elle aussi qui m'a prévenu que vous étiez prisonniers. »

D’un geste, Peter saute sur le bateau
et libère les enfants de leurs liens.
Les garçons grimpent en haut d’un mât
et se lancent dans la bataille.

**En équilibre sur la grande vergue,
Peter et Crochet dégainent
leurs armes et se battent.**

« Ne me tue pas, tu me regretterais, l'avertit le Capitaine pris au piège. Je ferai tout ce que tu voudras.

– Commence par dire que tu es un poisson pourri.

– **Je suis un poisson pourri.** »

À ces mots, Peter Pan saute de joie, et le pauvre Capitaine tombe…

« Mouche, à l'aide ! » gémit Crochet dans sa chute. Mais ni Mouche ni les pirates ne se préoccupent de leur Capitaine. Ils ont déjà sauté dans une chaloupe et prennent la fuite.

Seul le crocodile fait un excellent accueil au Capitaine... la gueule grande ouverte !

« Hip hip hip ! hourra ! s'écrient les enfants.
– Moussaillons ! levez l'ancre ! annonce Peter habillé en Capitaine.
– Mais, Peter, où allons-nous ? demande Wendy.
– Nous rentrons… à Londres. »

Peter fait signe à Clochette qui survole le bateau
et le recouvre peu à peu de **poussière magique.**
Ainsi, le navire s'élève dans les airs
sous les exclamations de joie des enfants.

À leur retour, M. et Mme Darling entrent dans la chambre des enfants pour s'assurer que tout va bien. « Wendy ! ma chérie ! » s'écrie Mme Darling en apercevant sa fille endormie près de la fenêtre.

La jeune fille ouvre les yeux. « Peter Pan vient de nous ramener du Pays Imaginaire ! **Maintenant, je suis prête à grandir !** »

« Ma petite fille, il y a un temps pour tout,
répond son père, de meilleure humeur.
– Georges ! l'interpelle soudain sa femme. Regarde ! »
Dans le ciel, un vaisseau s'éloigne lentement.

« C'est bizarre, j'ai l'impression d'avoir déjà vu ce navire,
chuchote M. Darling, ému et attendri.
C'était il y a bien longtemps... »